MANAGING THE INTERFACE:

Intergovernmental Affairs
Agencies in Canada

Bruce G. Pollard

Institute of
Intergovernmental Relations
Queen's University
Kingston, Ontario

Copyright 1986
ISBN 0-88911-448-X

Canadian Cataloguing in Publication Data

Pollard, Bruce G. (Bruce Gordon), 1955-
  Managing the interface : intergovernmental affairs
agencies in Canada

ISBN 0-88911-448-X

1. Federal-provincial relations - Canada.*
2. Administrative agencies - Canada. I. Queen's
University (Kingston, Ont.). Institute of Intergovernmental Relations. II. Title.

JL27.P64 1986   354.7108'2   C86-093386-5

CONTENTS

ACKNOWLEDGEMENTS

First and foremost, I would like to thank the officials in all thirteen governments (federal, provincial and territorial) who acted as my "contacts" for this study. These people gave of their time to discuss the issues here – both in person and by telephone; reviewed and commented upon relevant parts of the study; and supplied me with information and documents as needed. I extend a special word of appreciation to those officials who read and commented on an earlier draft of the complete manuscript. I would also like to thank the three former senior officials who played major roles in the development of intergovernmental affairs agencies in their respective governments for their willingness to talk with me about those events.

My colleagues at the Institute of Intergovernmental Relations have been most helpful in the preparation of this study. I am especially indebted to David Hawkes, Associate Director at the Institute, whose experience both in an intergovernmental affairs agency and in the academic world, give him an important insight into the subject of this study. His willingness to discuss at length the issues presented here, and his patience in reading over numerous drafts of this study, were crucial to getting this manuscript completed. Many of his ideas concerning intergovernmental agencies have been integrated into this book, especially the final chapter.

Special thanks go to my research assistant, Lloyd Hoffer, who spent many hours during the summer of 1985 poring over government documents and statutes in the libraries at Queen's University. Much of the information compiled for the profiles of the intergovernmental agencies is the result of his work.

Thanks to Peter Leslie, Director of the Institute, for his critical eye in focusing the scope of this study and for his comments on an earlier draft. Finally, thanks to Valerie Jarus for her diligence and patience in preparing this manuscript for publication, to Patricia Armson for her assistance on the word processor, to Andrea Purvis for applying her editing skills, and to Pauline Hawkes for her assistance on the publications front.

Bruce G. Pollard

INTRODUCTION

Hundreds of meetings every year. Thousands of informal contacts. Millions of dollars worth of agreements negotiated monthly. This is the nature of the interface among the federal, provincial and territorial governments in Canada. It is an active and complex relationship, reflecting a high degree of interdependence among governments. It is also a crucial element in the policy-making processes of all governments. Since all governments are dependent upon others in order to achieve some of their policy objectives, interdependence also introduces uncertainty into the process.

How have governments responded to this uncertainty and to this interdependence? How do governments manage the interface with other governments? The way in which governments organize themselves for handling their intergovernmental relations is the one element of control they can exercise in this uncertain world.

It was not intended that interdependence underlie Canadian federalism. In 1867, the architects of the British North America Act (now The Constitution Act, 1867) sought to distribute responsibilities between the two orders of government — federal and provincial — so that they would be able to function quite independently in their respective "watertight" compartments. Only two areas of concern — agriculture and immigration — were deemed to be the concurrent responsibility of both federal and provincial governments. However, as the report of the Royal Commission on the Economic Union and Development Prospects (the Macdonald Commission) notes: "Interdependence was a concern in 1867."[1] Because two orders of government are required to manage the federation, interdependence in Canadian federalism is inevitable.

Following the Second World War, the degree of interdependence increased dramatically as the scope of government activity penetrated most aspects of society. Canadian federalism in the post-war era can be divided into two periods. The first, dominating federal-provincial relations until the late 1950s, has been termed the period of "cooperative federalism." The second, which has existed for the past quarter-century, has been described as the period of "executive federalism."

Cooperative federalism was characterized by relations among governments that were narrow, functional and program-oriented. It has been termed "picket-fence" federalism, because most interaction occurred in narrow areas, with little effect on interaction in other sectors. Cooperative relations among technocrats dominated this period.

Executive federalism has been defined by Donald Smiley as "the relations between elected and appointed officials of the two orders of government in federal-provincial interactions".[2] The period of executive federalism is "characterized by the concentration and centralization of authority at the top of each participating government, the control and supervision of intergovernmental relations by politicians and officials with a wide range of functional interests, and the highly formalized and well-publicized proceedings of federal-provincial conference diplomacy."[3] It replaced "cooperative federalism" when federal-provincial relations became too broad, too important, too serious, and too political to be handled primarily by sectoral department officials.

The shift from cooperative to executive federalism had two major implications for the world of intergovernmental relations and for how governments organize for them.

With respect to the first, the volume of interaction among governments, the level at which it occurs and the nature of that interaction changed. There was an increase in the volume of interaction, particularly at the levels of senior officials and politicians. Meetings of deputy ministers, ministers, and first ministers dominate executive federalism. Because the key participants in intergovernmental liaison during the period of executive federalism are more senior than they were during cooperative federalism, the nature of the interaction is different as well. Generally, it is more political and more concerned with broader and higher profile issues.

The second major impact of the shift to the executive federalism period was a change in the institutional arrangements within governments. During the cooperative federalism period, it was officials within the sectoral departments who were involved in liaison with other governments. Towards the end of the 1950s, some departments that were heavily involved in intergovernmental affairs created special units to handle their interaction with other governments. As executive federalism began to dominate relations in the 1960s, governments in Canada developed new structures and machinery to manage their liaisons with other governments. In particular, central agencies for intergovernmental relations were created. These are the focus of this study.

The development of intergovernmental affairs agencies has at times been the subject of rather extensive criticism. These agencies have been accused of contributing to the level of conflict in federal-provincial relations; of distorting the priorities of governments; and of increasing the inefficiency within government. How accurate are these accusations? More importantly, how successful have intergovernmental affairs agencies been at enabling governments to manage the interface, to deal with the uncertainty that extensive interdependence has created?

This study will attempt to address these questions. Chapter One describes the development of intergovernmental affairs agencies in Canada, and discusses why all of the governments have created such agencies. Chapter Two examines the functions these agencies perform and the powers they exercise. Chapter Three attempts to explain the variation in structures, functions and powers among them, and the changes that have taken place within them. Chapter Four looks at the impact these agencies have made: first, on the intragovernmental world (relations within governments), and second, on their intergovernmental relations.

Finally, Chapter Five attempts to evaluate the intergovernmental affairs agencies. The most important criteria for evaluation is from the perspective of the governments that created them. Have these agencies fulfilled their purpose? Have they helped governments to meet their policy objectives in the intergovernmental realm? Equally important, are they essential for meeting the objectives of governments in the future?

In an Appendix at the end of this study, there is a series of profiles, describing the key intergovernmental affairs agency in each of the 13 governments (federal, provincial, and territorial) in Canada. Each profile summarizes the evolution of the agency, its statutory base (where one exists), its financial and human resources, the external offices for which it is responsible, and its mandate. There is also a list of formal intergovernmental affairs units that exist in other departments within the government, (that is, in departments other than the central intergovernmental affairs agency).

Notes

1. *Report of the Royal Commission on the Economic Union and Development Prospects for Canada. Volume 3,* Ottawa: Minister of Supply and Services, 1985, p. 20.
2. D.V. Smiley, *Canada in Question: Federalism in the Eighties. Third Edition,* Toronto: McGraw-Hill Ryerson Ltd., 1980, p. 91.
3. Garth Stevenson, *Unfulfilled Union. Canadian Federalism and National Unity. Revised Edition,* Toronto: Gage Publishing Ltd., 1982, pp. 190-1.

1 INTERGOVERNMENTAL AFFAIRS AGENCIES: A CANADIAN RESPONSE

An examination of the current intergovernmental landscape in Canada reveals a rather vast and complex web of structures and processes. There is an almost endless amount of interaction among all governments. The interface between governments has a variety of mechanisms for liaison. Some of these are formal, some informal. Some are committees which meet on a regular basis, others are purely *ad hoc*. Liaison takes place at several levels, involving first ministers, ministers, senior officials, or informal contact among line officials. Participants include, at times, the federal and all provincial and, perhaps, the territorial governments, a regional grouping of provincial governments, all the provinces, or the federal government and one or a small number of provinces. Finally, intergovernmental meetings cover a wide variety of issues and subject areas.

Because of the extensive volume of interaction with other governments, there has arisen within governments in Canada a need to "manage the interface" — to relate to other governments in Canada. There are a variety of possible institutional arrangements for accomplishing this. To visualize the scope of possible arrangements, it may be useful to employ a framework for analysis.

A Framework for Analysis

There are essentially three dimensions which together shape the way governments organize their intergovernmental relations. These are:

1. Structures
2. Functions and Powers
3. Resources

1. *Structures*

The first dimension, structural arrangements, has three elements:

- *location* of intergovernmental affairs units
    - formal intergovernmental affairs units within sectoral departments,
    - a distinct central agency for intergovernmental relations, or
    - both.
- *structural form* of intergovernmental affairs central agency (where one exists)
    - a unit in the office of the first minister or executive council,
        - reporting to the first minister; or
        - reporting to a separate minister;
    - a unit in the Finance or Treasury department;
    - a separate department,
        - with the first minister assuming responsibility; or
        - with a separate minister assuming responsibility.
- *external offices* which a government may operate, either in other jurisdictions within Canada or in other countries.

2. *Distribution of functions and powers*

The second dimension concerns "who does what" within a government with respect to its interaction with other governments. The distribution of both functions and powers is important in defining how governments organize their intergovernmental affairs. Of particular importance is the allocation of functions and powers related to intergovernmental liaison among:

- intergovernmental agencies,
- other central agencies,
- and line departments.

3. *Resources*
The level of resources, both financial and human, is the third dimension of the organization of intergovernmental relations. Two aspects need to be considered:

- the proportion of resources devoted to intergovernmental affairs
- the allocation of intergovernmental resources between intergovernmental central agencies and line department units.

It is important to note that the way in which governments organize their intergovernmental affairs involves specialized central agencies for intergovernmental affairs, as well as line departments and other central agencies. The creation of a separate unit for relations *between* governments, however, inevitably has implications for the relations *within* governments. This effect will be explored in Chapter Four.

Development of Structures for Managing the Interface
The way governments in Canada organize their intergovernmental affairs has changed dramatically in the 40 years since the Second World War. It was only in the mid-1950s that the first formal federal-provincial unit was created in a finance department. Currently, most finance and treasury departments, as well as numerous sectoral departments at both levels of government, contain formal federal-provincial units.

One of the effects of the rise of executive federalism during the 1960s and 1970s was the creation of intergovernmental affairs agencies to assist governments in managing the interface. No such agency existed before 1961. By 1980, all governments in Canada felt it necessary to structure their administration so that there was some focal point — be it an individual in the Executive Council Office of a small government, or a large full-fledged department — for intergovernmental relations.

Quebec was the first to establish a separate agency for intergovernmental affairs. In 1961, it created the Ministère des affaires fédérales-provinciales. This move followed the watershed election of 1960 which put Jean Lesage and the Liberal party into office. The previous Quebec government under Maurice Duplessis had often refused conditional grants from the federal government. It was argued that "the proliferation of specialized and fragmented intergovernmental relationships, such as those that arose from shared-cost programs, was a potential menace to the integrity of their provincial state and its ability or willingness to defend its own interests."[1] The Lesage government served notice that it would expect to receive its full share of benefits from Ottawa, but not at the expense of its provincial jurisdiction.

The creation of a separate department for federal-provincial affairs was integral to Quebec's new stance *vis à vis* Ottawa. The statute which created the department required the Minister of the department "to promote the full realization of provincial autonomy"[2] and to further intergovernmental collaboration in compliance with the constitution.

Six years later, the name of the department was changed to the *Ministère des affaires intergouver-nementales*. In 1974, the Act was amended, expanding the mandate of the department and enhancing the authority of the Minister. With respect to the latter, all intergovernmental agreements were to be signed by the Minister and no one was to take a position in the name of the government at an intergovernmental meeting unless authorized to do so by the Minister.

In 1974, the Department also assumed responsibility for international relations. In the ensuing years, two distinct branches developed: Canadian affairs and international affairs. In 1984, the domestic side of intergovernmental relations became a Secretariat in the *Ministère du Conseil Exécutif*, under the direction of a *Secrétaire générale associé*. After the election of the

Liberal Party in December 1985, a separate minister was given responsibility for both the *Secrétariat aux affaires intergouvernementales canadiennes* and the *Ministère des relations internationales.*

Following Quebec's lead, all other governments in Canada subsequently created units or departments to handle intergovernmental affairs. Although some of these agencies evolved through several structures, they all began as a unit either in the office of the first minister, or in the finance or treasury department.

Although an intergovernmental unit existed in the Alberta government's Executive Council Office prior to the 1971 general election, Peter Lougheed and the Progressive Conservative Party campaigned on a platform that included a promise to create an intergovernmental affairs department. Not surprisingly, the Department of Federal and Intergovernmental Affairs, which was created in the following year, was modelled quite closely on the Quebec example. It remains a strong and powerful central agency in the Alberta government.

Newfoundland established an Intergovernmental Affairs Secretariat in 1975 which, although part of the Executive Council Office, was similar in mandate and function to the departments that existed in Quebec and Alberta. The Secretariat was created by an Act of the Legislature which required that the minister responsible for the department sign all intergovernmental agreements. It remains a secretariat in the Executive Council Office.

At the federal level, the Federal-Provincial Relations Office (FPRO) was created in 1975, as part of the Privy Council Office. It evolved from the Federal-Provincial Relations Secretariat, which had been created in 1968, to serve the Cabinet Committee on Federal-Provincial Relations. Although this cabinet committee no longer exists, the FPRO remains a distinct entity, under the direction of a Secretary to the Cabinet for Federal-Provincial Relations, serving all cabinet committees and the Prime Minister directly on intergovernmental matters.

Saskatchewan created a Department of Intergovernmental Affairs in 1979. This department evolved from a unit that had existed in the Executive

Council Office since 1974. Its rise in status to a department under the responsibility of a senior minister reflected, to a great extent, the rise of constitutional negotiations on the public agenda. This department was different from its predecessors in Quebec and Alberta in that the minister had no statutory authority with respect to intergovernmental negotiations or agreements. Chapter Two will explore the relationship between the presence or absence of this statutory power, and the functions performed and the powers actually exercised by the intergovernmental affairs agency.

In 1983, a year after the election of the Progressive Conservatives in Saskatchewan, the Department of Intergovernmental Affairs was disbanded. An Intergovernmental Affairs Branch was created in the Executive Council Office. It is under the direction of an Associate Deputy Minister for Intergovernmental Affairs.

In 1979, both Nova Scotia and Prince Edward Island established Offices of Intergovernmental Affairs in their Executive Council Offices. Both were small and, in 1983, both were disbanded as part of a larger government reorganization. Nova Scotia no longer has a special unit for intergovernmental affairs. The Policy Board Secretariat has assumed these responsibilities under its much broader cloak. In Prince Edward Island, there remains an intergovernmental affairs unit within that government's Cabinet Office. A Deputy Secretary to Cabinet for Intergovernmental Affairs is the key official there.

New Brunswick has had a separate branch responsible for intergovernmental affairs in its Cabinet Secretariat since the mid-1970s. Currently, there is a Deputy Minister for Intergovernmental Affairs and Legislation and a small staff. This unit is concerned almost exclusively with the Government of New Brunswick's relations with other governments.

British Columbia created a Ministry of Intergovernmental Affairs in 1980. Previously, a unit had existed in the Premier's Office. This department is unique in that it doubles as a cabinet secretariat for all cabinet committees. The need for coordination and planning in all policy areas, not simply those related to interaction with other governments, and the pre-eminence of the constitution were the principal reasons for its creation.

Since 1980, the Yukon government has had, in turn, an intergovernmental affairs secretariat, a separate intergovernmental affairs department, an economic development and intergovernmental affairs department and, now, an intergovernmental affairs unit in the Executive Council Office. The Northwest Territories maintains a small intergovernmental relations office located in Ottawa.

Unlike Saskatchewan, Alberta, and British Columbia, where the intergovernmental affairs department evolved from a unit in their Executive Council Offices, an intergovernmental affairs agency in Ontario originated as a unit within the Treasury Department. In most governments, the first units specializing in intergovernmental relations were created in finance and treasury departments. These were developed in the 1950s and early 1960s at a time when intergovernmental relations were almost exclusively concerned with federal-provincial fiscal matters. Although the range of issues having a federal-provincial dimension has expanded dramatically, fiscal issues remain among the most important on the intergovernmental agenda. As such, the intergovernmental units in all finance or treasury departments are powerful elements in the bureaucracies of all governments in Canada.

Recognizing the link between fiscal and intergovernmental issues, in 1972 the Ontario government established the Ministry of Treasury, Economics and Intergovernmental Affairs. An intergovernmental affairs unit had been located in the Office of the Chief Economist since 1966. It was instrumental in developing the Confederation for Tomorrow Conference in 1967. In 1977, however, the government determined that an intergovernmental agency separate from the Treasury was desirable; the Ministry of Intergovernmental Affairs was subsequently created. The mandate and legislative authority of both the Ontario and the British Columbia departments are comparable to that which defined the Saskatchewan department.

Until 1983, Manitoba relied almost completely on the Federal-Provincial Relations and Research Division in the Department of Finance for all its intergovernmental expertise. This was comparable to the way in which the Ontario government organized its intergovernmental affairs during the mid-1970s. In 1983, a small intergovernmental affairs branch was created in the Executive Council Office, under a Deputy Secretary to Cabinet.

In summary, the current intergovernmental scene in Canada includes a wide variety of structures and forms which may be classified as intergovernmental affairs agencies. Two governments have departments of intergovernmental affairs with separate ministers. Quebec and Newfoundland have secretariats that function essentially as departments, with ministers other than the Premier. Ontario has a separate department, but the minister's role is currently assumed by the Premier. Six governments have clearly delineated units or personnel in the Premier's or the Executive Council Office (or the Privy Council Office, in the case of the federal government). In two governments, the intergovernmental agency serves as a secretariat to one or more cabinet committees. Only Nova Scotia no longer has a distinct central agency or unit concerned exclusively with intergovernmental affairs.

A variety of recent trends in the structure of intergovernmental affairs agencies in Canada can be highlighted. First, there has been a "rise and fall" of departments of intergovernmental relations: departments in the Yukon, Saskatchewan and Quebec governments no longer exist.

Second, this trend has been accompanied by an increasing centralization of intergovernmental affairs: in some governments, departments were replaced with units that were closer to the centre of power — the Executive Council Offices. This has occurred in the same three governments that have disbanded their departments: Quebec, Saskatchewan and Yukon. It can be argued that the status and power of the intergovernmental affairs specialists in each of these governments have been enhanced as a result of the changes. A related

12

development is the assumption of responsibility for intergovernmental relations in the cabinet by the premier or prime minister himself. This has recently occurred in Ontario, Nova Scotia and, for a few months, in Quebec.

Accompanying this centralization is an apparent increase in the politicization of the process. In recent years, there has been a tendency for members of the staffs of ministers and first ministers to play a greater role in intergovernmental negotiations and in determining intergovernmental policy. This could have important implications for intergovernmental central agencies in the future.

Concerning resources — both financial and human — there is no single trend across all governments regarding the level of resources allocated by a government to intergovernmental relations, or regarding the proportion of resources that governments put into intergovernmental affairs. For most governments, both the budgets and the number of personnel working in this area increased during the late 1970s and early 1980s. This was the era of the constitutional negotiation and patriation process.

Since the early 1980s, the budgets of most intergovernmental affairs agencies have levelled off somewhat, and some have actually declined. This may be partly a reflection of the restraint measures which all governments implemented during the years of the recession. In some governments, however, there has been a redirection of resources away from intergovernmental affairs agencies. Restructuring, which in some cases resulted in the outright elimination of a department or an office, has often meant that smaller agencies have become responsible for intergovernmental relations.

This brief history of how governments in Canada have organized their intergovernmental relations illustrates both the propensity for all governments to develop a central agency to serve as a focal point for their interaction with other governments, and the great variety in the nature of the agencies that have been created — both in structural terms and with respect to the power they hold and the roles they perform. Howard Leeson, former Deputy Minister of Intergovernmental Affairs in

Saskatchewan, notes both a similarity in the way governments in Canada have organized their intergovernmental affairs, and the great variation in the agencies adopted:

> The development of intergovernmental affairs agencies in Canada during the past two decades...involves broad institutional change and thus pressure for bureaucratic adjustment to respond to changing government roles in a decentralizing federation. But...it also reflects the autonomous tailoring of this development to individual needs as well as systemic pressures.[3]

Whether the intergovernmental affairs agencies adopted by governments across the country are more similar than varied is one theme that will underlie this study. Two questions surface:

1. Why have separate intergovernmental affairs agencies been created in all governments in Canada?
2. Why is there such a variety in the structural arrangements, functions, powers, and mandates of the intergovernmental agencies, and such a propensity for change within them?

The second question will be addressed in Chapter Three, which will explore the multitude of factors affecting the creation and evolution of intergovernmental affairs agencies in Canada. The remainder of Chapter One will look at the first question, following a very brief review of the situation in some other modern federations.

International Experience
In Australia, between 1974 and 1976, five of the six state governments and the Commonwealth government established units for monitoring and coordinating intergovernmental relations. All but one of these units are located in the Premier's (or Prime Minister's) office. The units are all small (between one and six staff) and most report to the first minister or to a separate minister responsible for relations with other governments.[4] These

agencies are similar, in many ways, to the intergovernmental affairs offices located in the Premier's Offices in some of the smaller Canadian provinces. They arose primarily because of increased interdependence and increased tension between state and Commonwealth governments. Their inception was also consistent with the move towards central control and strategic planning which was taking place in several of the governments.

In the United States, there are few structures parallel to the department or agency concerned with inter-governmental relations that has been established in every Canadian province. Milton Esman wrote in 1984 that in the United States, "federal-state relations are conducted primarily by numerous *ad hoc* linkages between program agencies in Washington and their counterparts in the states and cities."[5] State governments have not challenged federal supremacy or asserted competing claims on the loyalty of individuals or interest groups.

In their argument for limiting the amount of centrally coordinated federal-provincial machinery in Canada, Campbell and Szablowski look to Switzerland, with its ethnic and linguistic pluralism and strong regional and cantonal interest. The authors assert that any "attempt to establish in Bern a federal co-ordinating secretariat would be quickly dismissed on the grounds that it would only interfere with the relatively mutual federal-cantonal relations based on horizontal cooperation."[6]

The creation of specialized agencies or departments of intergovernmental affairs within the constituent governments of a federation has not been developed to the same extent outside Canada. National and regional governments in federations other than Canada seem to rely primarily on the functional contacts between officials in corresponding program departments. To the extent that intergovernmental relations exist, they are decentralized. Apart from Australia, there has been little or no effort to have a central agency coordinate a single position *vis à vis* other governments. The international situation suggests that the level of financial and human resources for intergovernmental affairs generally seems to be less than in Canada, and most of the resources that are allocated are fed into the program departments rather than into central agencies.

Explaining the Rise of Intergovernmental Affairs Agencies

There were primarily two factors which compelled governments in Canada (and to some extent, elsewhere) to develop intergovernmental affairs agencies. The first was the need for a government to coordinate its relations with other governments. The second was the rise of cross-departmental issues on the intergovernmental agenda.

The Need for Coordination

The creation of intergovernmental affairs agencies and the growth of intergovernmental machinery generally is due primarily to two factors: the increase in the scope of government activity and the resulting interdependence of federal and provincial governments in virtually every policy area.[7] Governments of all western liberal democracies dramatically expanded their activities in the post-war period as they entered vast new areas of policy. For federal countries, this growth in government activity has led to greater interaction among governments. The increase in areas of shared responsibility has led to "vastly overlapping and intricately interlocked policy spaces."[8]

The increased interdependence of governments in Canada is enhanced by particular aspects of the Canadian situation; these tend to ensure the increased entanglement of governments. One such characteristic is the imbalance between the constitutional allocation of responsibilities and resources on one hand, and the demands on government on the other. The issue of fiscal transfers between governments has been an item on the intergovernmental agenda almost since Confederation.

Ronald Burns noted that the fundamental purpose of intergovernmental cooperation is to adjust those areas of "governmental power and responsibility which do not correspond to the constitutional definition, either through the inability to define them or through changing circumstances."[9] Donald Smiley wrote in 1964: "Within the existing division of powers and responsibilities between the federal and provincial governments, there are too many ways in which the activities of one level can vitally affect the interests and objectives of the other to make tolerable a situation in which policies are decided upon and implemented unilaterally."[10]

The interdependence of governments in Canada has become even more prevalent in the past two decades, as both levels of government have sought to develop comprehensive economic policies. The policies of one government at either level can have major implications for the national economy. A coordinated approach to national economic management is no longer simply desirable – it is essential.

The impact of this interdependence has affected the organization within governments. "The growth of the state and of interdependence gives rise to new requirements for managing relations between governments."[11] Audrey Doerr observes that by the 1970s, the size and complexity of governments in Canada had advanced to the point that specialists were needed to manage the processes of intergovernmental co-ordination.[12] As a result, governments have created central agencies for this purpose. Seymour Wilson observes that in addition to large expenditure areas which required substantial interaction – such as regional development, health, and employment – there was also regulatory conflict, which was often located outside the realm of regular departments. "It is little wonder that the need was felt that some visible new organizational form would be created to effect proper coordination"[13] at both the federal and provincial levels.

There are different motives related to coordination for which intergovernmental affairs agencies were created. First is the goal of coherence and consistency which became increasingly difficult with the growing interdependence of governments. There are several hundred intergovernmental agreements in force, involving numerous government departments and accounting for millions of dollars. Most governments believe it is essential that there be one agency which monitors the breadth of interface between itself and other governments.

17

This need for coordination became especially apparent during the 1960s and the 1970s with the increased importance of regional development policy. The federal-provincial shared-cost agreement was the central policy instrument in this area. In varying degrees across the country, shared-cost agreements were reached between federal line departments and their provincial counterparts. While these gave large sums of federal money to a province, they also committed a large proportion of provincial funds to particular projects and sectors. The more agreements that were signed and the smaller the fiscal size of the province, the greater the impact that these agreements had on provincial government priorities. As a result, it became imperative for smaller governments that were heavily involved in cost-shared agreements to have some central coordination of these agreements. This was one important impetus for the creation of the Intergovernmental Affairs Secretariat in Newfoundland in 1974.

The effect of these cost-shared agreements was not the same for all provinces; the impact has been more important for the smaller and poorer provinces than for the larger and richer. For the provinces in the latter group, fewer agreements have been signed and the funds for such accords account for a much smaller proportion of their provincial budgets. For example, even though the Department of Federal and Intergovernmental Affairs in Alberta assumes responsibility for that province's regional development agreements, it cannot be said that the necessity of their coordination was a primary reason for its creation.

A second motive for a government coordinating its relations with other governments was to ensure that it was aware of relevant developments and policy decisions in other governments. This was especially important in provinces that relied heavily on federal funding. Some governments argue that the existence of intergovernmental affairs specialists has helped them to get more from their interaction with other governments. The central coordination of intergovernmental affairs enables a government's interaction to be much more systematic and comprehensive. In establishing an Office of Intergovernmental Relations in Nova Scotia in 1979, Premier Buchanan noted that the absence of such an office had forced the province into taking "a piecemeal approach to federal assistance programs." The Premier stated: "I have every reason to believe that we have missed opportunities to take full advantage of many of the federal government's financial assistance programs."[14]

Third, it has been suggested by some analysts that the need for coordination within the provincial governments arose, at least partly, as a defense mechanism. Anthony Careless notes that the lack of cohesion among provincial departments when they negotiated with the new "horizontal" federal departments (for example, the Department of Regional and Economic Expansion) meant that Ottawa could often play one department against another, and succeed in getting favourable, isolated agreements that collectively jeopardized the development of the economy according to the province's goals.[15]

Finally, it has been suggested that for some governments, the defense of constitutional jurisdiction was a primary impetus behind the coordination of intergovernmental activity. Some have argued that the need for coordination increases with the level of dissatisfaction within the federation, or with the level of conflict and acrimony *vis à vis* the other order of government. Intergovernmental coordination in periods of conflict versus periods of cooperation is a theme that will be explored later in this study.

How does the need to coordinate affect the way a government organizes? Clearly, it gives a certain power and responsibility to a central agency or other unit at the centre, which is situated so that it can survey the entire breadth of interaction. As well, it bestows some power so that this agency can influence the decision-making process, or have some control over policies being pursued by the sectoral departments. However, the nature of the agency or mechanism that a government adopts to orchestrate this coordination has varied greatly from government to government.

The Nature of the Public Agenda

Beyond the need for coordination, the nature of the public agenda in recent years has compelled some governments to establish central agencies for intergovernmental affairs. Many of the issues on the recent intergovernmental agenda do not fall neatly within the scope of individual departments. Rather, they are "cross-departmental" in nature. Two such areas of public policy, which were prominent during the 1970s, are the constitution and regional development. Both involve a spectrum of policy sectors, and the presence of both on the agenda played an important role in enhancing the importance of intergovernmental affairs agencies in all jurisdictions. The need for coordination which arises from regional development policy has already been discussed.

With respect to constitutional issues, it can be argued that these enhanced the status of intergovernmental affairs units which, to some extent, became "departments of the constitution". These agencies effectively became line departments, employing personnel who were specialists in constitutional matters.

The need for separate agencies at the centre to handle the constitutional issue seems to be rooted in two factors. First, the issue was clearly "cross-departmental". Virtually everything was on the table during the constitutional negotiations which commenced in 1978. There was no obvious single agency to handle the issue. Second, the constitutional issue was of critical importance to all governments. For some first ministers, it was important that the issue be handled by an agency close to them.

Furthermore, there seems to be a constitutional aspect to nearly every important issue. As a result, in some governments, it has been the constitutional experts, often located in the intergovernmental affairs agencies rather than in the sectoral or Attorney-General/Justice Departments, that have played a key role in the intergovernmental aspects of certain issues.

An example is provided by the Government of Newfoundland. There, the Intergovernmental Affairs Secretariat played the lead role in negotiations with the federal government over offshore oil. (At the federal

20

level, this role was assumed by the Department of Energy, Mines and Resources.) Although the decision to give the lead role to the Intergovernmental Affairs Secretariat was partly a decision based on the capabilities and expertise of the individuals involved, it also signified that this was an issue where the constitutional question was of utmost importance. A corollary to this argument is that the role of intergovernmental agencies is diminished to some extent when the constitutional aspect of an issue is not in question.

This discussion has sought to give a "broad brush" explanation of the development of intergovernmental affairs agencies in Canadian governments. The wide variation among the agencies has, for the most part, not been considered. The next two chapters will explore these. Chapter Two will describe the functions performed and the powers exercised by intergovernmental affairs agencies in Canada. Chapter Three will examine the multitude of factors which, together, help to explain the unique developments in each jurisdiction.

Notes

1. Garth Stevenson, *Unfulfilled Union. Canadian Federalism and National Unity. Revised Edition*, Toronto: Gage Publishing Ltd., 1982, p. 192.
2. Statutes of Quebec. *An Act to Establish the Department of Federal-Provincial Affairs*, 24 March 1961, section 3.
3. Howard Leeson, "Accommodative Mechanisms in a Decentralizing Federation: The Intergovernmental Affairs Function in Saskatchewan." Presented to the Institute for Public Administration, St. John's, 30 August 1985, pp. 1-2.
4. John Warhurst, "Intergovernmental Managers and Co-operative Federalism: The Australian Case." *Public Administration*, Vol. 61, 1983, p. 312.
5. Milton J. Esman, "Federalism and Modernization: Canada and the United States." *Publius. The Journal of Federalism*. 14:1 (Winter 1984), p. 30.

6. C. Campbell and G. Szablowski, *The Superbureaucrats: Structure and Behaviour in Central Agencies*. Toronto: Macmillan of Canada, 1979, p. 236.
7. Richard Simeon, "Intergovernmental Relations in Canada Today - Summary of Discussions." in R. Simeon, ed. *Confrontation and Collaboration - Intergovernmental Relations in Canada Today*. Toronto: The Institute of Public Administration of Canada, 1979. p. 4.
8. Charles Goodsell, "The Role and Importance of Bureaucracy in Federal Systems." Prepared for Royal Australian Institute of Public Administration, Perth, Australia, November 1984, p. 7.
9. R.M. Burns, *Intergovernmental Liaison on Fiscal and Economic Matters*. Kingston: Institute of Intergovernmental Relations, 1968, p. 54.
10. Donald V. Smiley, "Public Administration and Canadian Federalism." *Canadian Public Administration*. VII:3, 1964, p. 385.
11. *Report of the Royal Commission on the Economic Union and Development Prospects for Canada. Volume 3*, Ottawa: Minister of Supply and Services, 1985, p. 15.
12. Audrey Doerr, "Public Administration: Federalism and Intergovernmental Relations." in K. Kernaghan, ed. *Canadian Public Administration: Discipline and Profession*. Toronto: Butterworths, 1983, p. 132.
13. Seymour V. Wilson, "Federal-Provincial Relations and Federal-Policy Processes, in Doern and Aucoin, ed. *Public Policy in Canada*. Toronto: the Macmillan Company of Canada, 1979, p. 209.
14. Government of Nova Scotia. *House of Assembly Debates and Proceedings*, 6 April 1979, p. 1602.
15. Anthony Careless, *Initiative and Response. The Adaptation of Canadian Federalism to Regional Economic Development*. Montreal: The Institute of Public Administration of Canada, 1977, p. 145.

2 FUNCTIONS AND POWERS

One of the primary questions this study seeks to answer is: "What is the role of the intergovernmental affairs agency?" There is a rather extensive list of functions performed by these agencies in governments across Canada. The list includes functions related to coordination goals, perhaps the central reason for their creation. Other functions involve providing a service to different clients within government; assuming the lead responsibility on particular issues; and playing a key role in the government's international activities.

Intricately related to an agency's functions are the powers it exercises. Certain activities provide some intergovernmental agencies with an element of power, but powers vary among agencies. For example, it may have very strict control, whereby any interaction with other governments by a line department must be approved by it, or it may simply play an advisory role, providing information to the policy makers in the line departments.

FUNCTIONS

Following is a list of functions performed by at least some of the intergovernmental agencies in Canada. They are divided into four general categories:

1. Coordination/Control Function
   a. monitoring of sectors
   b. participation in intergovernmental meetings
   c. negotiating and signing of agreements
   d. screening of proposals for cabinet
   e. intergovernmental policy development
   f. administration of external affairs (domestic)
2. Service Function
   a. service to first ministers
   b. service to other departments
   c. cabinet secretariat functions
3. Lead Responsibility
   a. constitutional issues
   b. cross-departmental issues
   c. residual policy issues
   d. "hot" political issues
4. International Relations
   a. coordination of government's international activities
   b. administration of external offices (international)
   c. protocol functions

The next section examines more closely each of these functions as they are performed by intergovernmental affairs agencies. The description of each includes examples from some of the governments. A more complete list of functions performed by each agency in all governments is provided in the profiles of the agencies in the Appendix.

Coordination
In his 1968 study, Ronald Burns observed that:

> some coordinating unit should exist and should be placed in the special position which will enable it to deal with those matters of mutual involvement in a way that will eliminate much of the confusion which has been so typical of the situation in the past without interfering with the established flow of business which is carried on directly between federal and provincial departments. [1]

Coordination was defined in 1970 by Donald Smiley as the process by which a complex set of public activities is ordered according to some set of goals or priorities.[2] It relates both to the ranking itself and subsequent actions to implement these decisions.

Coordination involves some imposition of policy or objectives from the centre onto the line departments. Intergovernmental affairs agencies generally seek to ensure that intergovernmental policies of the various departments within the government are consistent with the general objectives of the government as a whole. How that is handled and the degree to which it is effective varies from government to government.

Obtaining information is critical to coordination. The first function of a central agency in its efforts to coordinate is "monitoring" – the act of gathering information. A second, and related function is participation in intergovernmental sectoral meetings. How much information an agency receives, and the nature of that information, will affect its capacity to coordinate. For some intergovernmental agencies, coordination involves no more than a rather loose monitoring of policies in all sectors, with an eye to anything that is out of step with the government's general direction. Monitoring in itself does not enable a government to "coordinate." It is important to notice the direction of the information flow. Here, it goes from the departments to the centre. Coordination, however, implies some control. This necessarily involves an attempt to impose direction from the centre onto policies emanating from the line departments.

Two of the more easily measured forms of control are the negotiation and signing of agreements and the screening of proposals to cabinet. In varying degrees, intergovernmental affairs agencies perform these two functions. The final, and the most potent function of coordination performed by agencies in some of the governments, is the development of their government's intergovernmental policy and strategy.

Monitoring of Sectors

Intergovernmental affairs agencies are involved in monitoring developments across policy sectors, both within their own government and within other governments. The first involves communicating with the line departments. Much of this liaison is informal. The larger intergovernmental affairs departments employ officers who have a "portfolio" of line departments to monitor. In other governments, the relationship between the intergovernmental central agency and the departments is less structured.

Agencies vary in the extent to which they monitor policy sectors. In some governments, the agencies try to keep abreast of the intergovernmental aspects in virtually all policy sectors. This involves regular contact with virtually all departments and often attending intergovernmental meetings of officials and ministers in specific sectoral areas. Large departments of intergovernmental affairs, such as those that exist in Ontario, British Columbia and Alberta, try to monitor policy sectors on such a comprehensive scale.

Governments with smaller intergovernmental offices make no attempt to be as comprehensive. The intergovernmental affairs specialists in these governments, most often located in the Executive Council Office, tend to monitor an issue closely only if affairs do not function smoothly, or when an issue attains a high political profile.

The information flows from the departments to the centre. In some governments, such as Alberta, the administrative process ensures that the intergovernmental agency receives relevant documents, such as copies of correspondence and background papers. In others, though, there is no compelling reason for departments to forward such information to the central agency, and the agency may receive information in a sporadic fashion.

Monitoring can assist an intergovernmental affairs agency in determining if the government is consistent in its approach to intergovernmental affairs across all policy sectors. This is the first step in the coordination function.

Another aspect of the monitoring function involves the linking of issues. In his description of the situation in the Saskatchewan government, Howard Leeson writes that in the late 1970s, it was realized that there was considerable importance in managing the overall relationship of the province with other jurisdictions. "It was a realization that these relations were not simply discrete negotiations or issues, but also had in their totality some political importance."[3] Governments vary in the degree to which they link issues.

In addition to monitoring the various policy sectors within their own governments, some intergovernmental agencies also track developments in other governments. Large intergovernmental bureaucracies, such as those that exist in Alberta and Ontario, expend substantial resources monitoring developments in other governments. Provincial agencies monitor legislation in other provinces. As well, they often monitor federal developments in order to discern an overall approach on the part of the federal government towards intergovernmental relations. They may seek information about financial assistance possibilities from the federal government.

Monitoring developments in other governments not only provides additional, and potentially useful, information for a government, but it also develops personal contacts among officials in the intergovernmental agencies. Kenneth Kernaghan notes that an essential attribute of intergovernmental specialists is their ability to obtain current information on the perceptions and positions of other governments.[4] This ability comes largely from the development of a network of personal contacts among officials in intergovernmental agencies, based on respect and trust.

Participation in Intergovernmental Meetings
There are two categories of intergovernmental meetings that central agency officials often attend. First are those concerned with the planning and preparation of First Ministers' and Premiers' Conferences. Officials from intergovernmental affairs agencies in all governments generally attend these meetings. More will be said about these in a later section.

Second are meetings of officials or ministers from corresponding sectoral departments in two or more governments. Often, only representatives from the larger intergovernmental agencies attend these meetings. There are various roles that the intergovernmental affairs specialists who do attend these sectoral meetings play. Some officials are there as "policemen", ensuring that positions stated by the representatives from the line department do not diverge from the overall government approach. A second role is to point out linkages between the policy issue at hand and other sectors. A third role is to report back to the first minister on both the substance and tone of the meeting, and on the positions taken by other governments. Some intergovernmental agency representatives perform more than one of these functions.

Negotiation and Signing of Agreements
One method of control by a central agency relates to the signing of intergovernmental agreements. In the Governments of Alberta, Quebec, and Newfoundland, intergovernmental agreements must be signed by the minister responsible for intergovernmental affairs in order to be valid. These governments all have large intergovernmental affairs departments or secretariats with their powers specified in legislation.

Although Ontario and British Columbia also have statutory-based departments of intergovernmental affairs, there is no requirement that agreements with other governments be signed by the Ministers of these departments. In 1978, officials from the Ministry of Intergovernmental Affairs in Ontario drafted a proposed set of regulations, which stipulated that their agency be a party to all intergovernmental discussions and agreements. It was assailed by representatives of the program ministries at an inter-ministry meeting and was not adopted.[5] Similarly in Saskatchewan, although the legislation which created the Department of Intergovernmental Affairs stipulated that the Minister *may* be a party to the negotiation of agreements and was authorized to sign intergovernmental agreements, it explicitly stated that the failure to comply with these and other provisions did *not* render the agreement inoperative.

The situation in the territorial governments is somewhat different. The intergovernmental affairs agency in the Yukon government's Executive Council Office now co-signs (with the line department) all intergovernmental agreements. However, intergovernmental agreements involving either the Government of the Yukon or the Government of the Northwest Territories must also be signed by the appropriate Commissioner of the Territory (a federal government appointee).

In practice, the functions performed by the three agencies having legislative power over the signing of agreements may not vary much from the agencies in other governments. In Ontario, for example, it is administrative policy for line departments to have the Ministry of Intergovernmental Affairs review and co-sign significant intergovernmental agreements. This has been reconfirmed by the new Premier. Although there is no legislative "cudgel", there is generally cooperation from the departments. In Saskatchewan, prior to 1983, the Minister of Intergovernmental Affairs had to see each agreement before it received Cabinet approval. It is often advisable for a line department to obtain the consent of the intergovernmental affairs central agency before a policy is sent to cabinet, even if it is not required by statute.

Conversely, while it may be required that an agency co-sign all agreements with other governments, the amount of input and influence (that is, power) which the agency actually has with respect to the negotiation of agreements may vary substantially. The presence of legislation giving certain powers to an intergovernmental affairs agency does not necessarily mean that power, especially over line departments, always resides with that agency. While legislative authority is one indicator of power, it is not the sole indicator.

Screening of Proposals for Cabinet
Intergovernmental affairs agencies can also exercise some control by screening proposals and documents which go to cabinet, to ensure that they are consistent with the

government's overall objectives in intergovernmental affairs. Virtually all agencies have some screening capacity, although it is a more formal process in some governments than in others, such that cabinet proposals having an intergovernmental impact are automatically routed to the agency.

In Alberta, for example, Requests for Decisions (RFDs) often include an assessment of intergovernmental impact before going to cabinet. The Department of Federal and Intergovernmental Affairs screens those RFDs that have an impact on federal-provincial relations. In Ontario, the Deputy Minister of Intergovernmental Affairs receives all cabinet documents directly from the Cabinet Office. While he has always been able to acquire these, the link is much more direct now that the Premier is also the Minister of Intergovernmental Affairs. Moreover, that government's "manual of administration" states that if a department is involved in an intergovernmental issue, it is to consult both the Treasury Department and the Ministry of Intergovernmental Affairs for advice. In the federal government of Brian Mulroney, departments must ensure that the Federal-Provincial Relations Office is consulted where federal-provincial relations could be implicated as a result of some policy decision. [6]

In many of the smaller governments, where the agency is located in the Executive Council Office or the Premier's Office, the process is less formal. Because of their location, these units have access to, and are able to advise on submissions to cabinet. In New Brunswick, Manitoba, and Prince Edward Island, for example, the absence of legislation does not signal the absence of control over intergovernmental affairs. There is a unit, – in some instances, it is only one individual – who screens cabinet proposals for their potential intergovernmental impact. This unit or individual is very close to the Premier, and has the power that accrues from that proximity. There is no legislation giving the agency or individual instruments of control – it is not needed.

Intergovernmental Policy Development
The development of a government's intergovernmental policy and strategy can be the most powerful coordinating function that an intergovernmental affairs agency performs. Power is exercised to the extent that the policy developed in these agencies actually "directs" the government's strategy and approach in intergovernmental relations.

Some intergovernmental affairs agencies maintain a unit that concentrates on developing broad, government-wide positions and approaches to intergovernmental relations. Specialists in these units operate on a longer time frame than most policy advisors. They are concerned with the "corporate image" of the government. According to Timothy Woolstencroft, Ontario's Ministry of Intergovernmental Affairs (MIA), at least in the early 1980s, had only minimal involvement in formulating Ontario's intergovernmental strategies and policies, with the exception of constitutional issues.[7] Evidence suggests that since creating a "policy development" unit in MIA, the Ministry's impact on Ontario's intergovernmental strategy has been enhanced from a reactive to a proactive stance. Other governments with such a unit in their intergovernmental affairs agencies include British Columbia, Alberta and Quebec.

Administration of External Offices (Domestic)
Various types of external offices have been created by governments in Canada. There are provincial and territorial government offices located in the national capital, in other provinces, and in foreign countries. This last category of provincial offices will be discussed in a later section. A final category comprises federal offices in provincial capitals.

The provinces of British Columbia, Alberta, Saskatchewan, Ontario and Quebec maintain offices in Ottawa. These generally serve a variety of functions. Perhaps most important is the "Ottawa watch" function — monitoring events, maintaining contacts, and watching for early warning signals of federal policies. This function can only be properly accomplished by having someone in the national capital on a continual basis. For all provincial governments, the relationship with the federal government is by far their most important intergovernmental link.

Donald Stevenson, former Deputy Minister of the Ministry of Intergovernmental Affairs in Ontario, and now that province's senior representative in Ottawa and Quebec City, argued in 1979 for permanent provincial offices in Ottawa to help overcome the lack of continuity and fragmentation which exists in the system. He argued that these could eliminate the need for many of the intergovernmental meetings which were held solely for the purpose of disseminating information.[8] An annual report of Alberta's Department of Federal and Intergovernmental Affairs is careful to note, however, that the "Ottawa office does not replace direct communication between the Alberta government and the federal government."[9] The three western provinces have had offices in Ottawa for several years. Quebec has had a small Ottawa *bureau* since 1984. Ontario established a permanent office in the national capital in 1985, after a trial period of one year.

Both the Yukon and the Northwest Territories have offices in Ottawa. These serve a unique function, partly because of the geographic distance between the territorial capitals and Ottawa, and partly because of the relationship they have with the federal government. Unlike the provincial offices located in Ottawa, which serve to complement the intergovernmental affairs departments or agencies based in the provincial capitals, the Northwest Territories' office in Ottawa *is* the main intergovernmental unit for the government. There is no agency located in Yellowknife. Similarly in the Yukon, although there is an Intergovernmental Affairs Secretariat in Whitehorse, the Federal Relations Office in Ottawa often acts as a devolved part of the Secretariat. For example, it often sends representatives to intergovernmental meetings and acts in other ways on behalf of the Yukon government.

Some provincial and territorial governments have external offices in parts of the country other than the national capital. Quebec has offices in three cities in other provinces: Toronto, Moncton and Edmonton. These serve various purposes, including the promotion of economic opportunities and the maintenance of cultural links with the francophone communities in the other provinces. The Government of the Northwest Territories has an office in Edmonton, primarily for the purpose of serving the public. Edmonton is the main link between the Northwest Territories and the rest of the country.

Another category of external office is the federal government office located within the provinces. Currently, there is a federal Economic Development Coordinator (FEDC) in each province. Originally created with the Ministry of State for Economic and Regional Development (MSERD) in 1982, the FEDCs replaced the provincial Directors-General of the now disbanded Department of Regional and Economic Expansion. When Prime Minister John Turner disbanded MSERD in 1984, the FEDCs became part of the Department of Regional Industrial Expansion (DRIE).

> The FEDC was to ensure that a 'decentralized central agency' would be present in the field and would encourage all federal departments to 'tailor' their policies and programs to correspond to the economic circumstances of the respective provinces.[10]

The FEDC system put into place "an official who not only had some power to facilitate cooperation among federal line departments and agencies within the regions, but who was also to communicate and coordinate the implementation of government decisions within the regions."[11] In this respect, FEDCs perform what are essentially central agency functions. In their paper for the Royal Commission on the Economic Union and Development Prospects for Canada, Aucoin and Bakvis recommend that FEDCs be attached to the Federal-Provincial Relations Office.[12]

Service Function
All intergovernmental affairs agencies play an important "service" role to a variety of clients. There are three

general categories of clients: the first minister; sectoral line departments; and cabinet committees.

Service to First Ministers
In his 1968 study, Ronald Burns observed that: "so important are the questions of intergovernmental involvement that any central authority must be directly responsible to the office of the first minister and not merely be another department of government."[13] Since that was written, some governments have given responsibility for intergovermental relations to ministers other than the first minister. However, all intergovernmental affairs units, including those with a separate departmental structure and minister, have found that a substantial amount of the work they do is directly for their premier or prime minister. Peter Meekison, former Deputy Minister of the Department of Federal and Intergovernmental Affairs (FIGA) in Alberta, estimates that one-third of FIGA's time is spent in work directly for the premier.[14] In explaining the rationale for disbanding the Department of Intergovernmental Affairs in Saskatchewan and the creation of a distinct unit in the Executive Council Office in 1983, then Finance Minister Robert Andrews noted that the department had often dealt "on a premier-to-premier level" and that was being reflected in the structural changes.[15]

A key aspect of service to the first minister involves the preparation for intergovernmental meetings in which he is participating. As such, the greater the number of first ministers' meetings, the greater the amount of time that the intergovernmental affairs' officials must spend in preparation. The following conferences involving first ministers are held annually: Annual Premiers' Conferences (APCs), Western Premiers' Conferences (WPCs) and Maritime Premiers/New England Governors' Conferences. As well, the Council of Maritime Premiers (CMPs) meets at least four times a year. In recent years, First Ministers' Conferences (FMCs) have generally been held once or twice annually.

The First Ministers' Conference is "the apex of Canadian summitry."[16] Since Confederation, there have been 61 such conferences, 41 of these since 1960. At the

February 1985 Conference, held in Regina, the FMC was "institutionalized" in that all provincial premiers, as well as the Prime Minister, agreed to hold an FMC to discuss major intergovernmental issues annually for the ensuing five years. This introduced a degree of predictability into the system, enabling intergovernmental support agencies to prepare for such conferences in a more systematic fashion than has often been the case in the past.

Many of the FMCs during the late 1970s and early 1980s were related to the constitution. Since the historic meeting of November 1981 – when a partial accord was signed by the Prime Minister and nine of the provincial premiers, leading to the proclamation of the Canadian constitution in April 1982 – constitutional issues have not been at the centre of the intergovernmental agenda. However, three FMCs have been held since 1982 – and a further one is scheduled for 1987 – on constitutional reform as it relates to aboriginal matters. These meetings of first ministers were unique in Canadian history, in that they included not only the prime minister and premiers of all ten provinces, but also the government leaders from the two territories, and the leaders of Canada's major national aboriginal organizations.

Premiers have met annually since 1960. A principal advocate of interprovincial cooperation was Jean Lesage of Quebec, elected in 1960. Until 1974, federal observers were invited to these meetings. However, because some premiers felt that the meetings had developed into a performance for the benefit of the federal government, it was decided that henceforth, federal observers would not be invited. Since 1982, the government leaders from the two territories have been invited as observers.

The Council for Maritime Premiers, which includes the premiers of Nova Scotia, New Brunswick, and Prince Edward Island, was established in May 1971, and meets four times per year. A "steering committee", which includes a senior intergovernmental official from each of the three governments, meets on several occasions to prepare for these meetings. In addition, members of this steering committee are also part of a committee which meets about four times per year to prepare for the annual conference of Maritime Premiers and New England Governors.

The Western Premiers' Conference began in 1965 as the Prairie Economic Council, composed of Manitoba, Saskatchewan, and Alberta. British Columbia was invited to join in March 1973, and the name was changed to the Western Economic Council. The following year, it became the Western Premiers' Conference, and the four western premiers have usually met once a year since then.[17]

Specific duties related to the preparation of meetings involving first ministers include: the determination of the agenda (in concert with officials from other governments) and the preparation of the "briefing books" for the first minister. Although the relevant departments (depending on the agenda) usually write the briefing notes, intergovernmental affairs officials are often required to rewrite and edit them, and to write broad summaries and overviews. Moreover, in some governments, these central agency officials write their government's position papers and briefing notes with respect to broader intergovernmental issues, such as "duplication", regional development, and constitutional issues. Perhaps most importantly, intergovernmental officials often write their government's strategic overview for a conference.

A second aspect of the service function, as it relates to the first minister, involves monitoring issues across the spectrum of policy sectors. It was noted earlier that "monitoring" is the first stage in coordinating intergovernmental policy. In some intergovernmental agencies, monitoring is done primarily for the purpose of keeping the premier or prime minister abreast of what is happening in the world of intergovernmental affairs on a day-to-day basis. The extent to which a first minister requires a unit to perform this duty is largely a function of the size of government and its degree of decentralization. Monitoring is more likely to be required in a large and decentralized government, such as the federal government. This is an important function performed by the Federal-Provincial Relations Office (FPRO) in its role of serving the prime minister.

Advising the first minister on intergovernmental policy and strategy is a third way in which intergovernmental

36

agencies serve the first minister. The Deputy Minister of the Department of Federal and Intergovernmental Affairs (FIGA) during the 1970s and early 1980s, for example, often directly advised the Premier on key intergovernmental issues, such as energy, Established Programs Financing, and the constitution. This advice was given, even though the Deputy Minister was directly responsible to a Minister other than the Premier. The extent to which this role is played by officials from intergovernmental affairs agencies depends largely on personalities and on the ability of an agency to engage in strategic planning. FIGA has the capacity to provide strategic planning with respect to federal-provincial relations. Similarly, there is evidence that in Ontario, the role of the Ministry of Intergovernmental Affairs (MIA) has been enhanced since the election of the Peterson government — a government which considers strategic planning to be important. Like FIGA, MIA has this capacity with respect to intergovernmental policy.

Audrey Doerr writes that one of the principal functions of the FPRO has been to provide the prime minister and cabinet with assistance in examining federal-provincial issues of current and long-term concern.[18] In the House of Commons discussion on the bill which created the office of Secretary to the Cabinet for Federal-Provincial Relations, the Honourable Martin O'Connell stated:

> The office [FPRO] will be reporting to the Prime Minister giving him the advice and support with which he can coordinate the activities of the other ministers who have more specialized jurisdictions in this particular area.[19]

Service to Other Departments

Intergovernmental affairs agencies often perform services for other departments in the government. For the most part, this involves keeping sectoral departments informed with respect to what is happening on the intergovernmental front in their sector and other sectors, and with respect to the government's overall approach to intergovernmental affairs. For example, Ontario's

Ministry of Intergovernmental Affairs (MIA) uses a weekly newsletter, an annual review of current and future intergovernmental issues, and presentations to officials in sectoral departments to fulfill this function.

Although it is difficult to measure, this service function can also be a source of power. Power can be accrued through expertise and a proven "track record". Most intergovernmental affairs agencies were initially mistrusted by line departments. Over time, though, in most of the governments, they have been able to prove themselves and to show line departments that they have a positive role to play. An intergovernmental affairs unit has attained a large measure of power when it is able to offer a credible alternate strategy with respect to a department's intergovernmental affairs, and when that department acts on the advice.

A special type of service performed by some intergovernmental agencies is policy analysis and development for some of the sectoral departments. The extent to which this is done varies considerably across the broad range of sectoral departments in any government. Often a department which is responsible for a sector that is only recently involved in intergovernmental issues will rely heavily on the intergovernmental central agency for its strategic planning in these matters. However, most of these departments tend to develop their own expertise over time. The Department of Fisheries in Newfoundland, and the Department of Energy in Ontario are examples of departments that initially relied on the central agency, but have since developed their own expertise in intergovernmental issues.

Officials in intergovernmental agencies in some governments often assist sectoral departments in their federal-provincial negotiations. With respect to some issues, they may communicate the positions of other departments and governments which may be directly or indirectly affected. Donald Wallace argues that the primary concern of provincial intergovernmental agencies with respect to the discussions on the *Young Offenders Act*, for example, was to make sure that when the issue was raised, the province spoke with one voice.[20] He suggests that the potential for a government's position to disintegrate is high without careful internal coordination.

Cabinet Secretariat Functions
Some intergovernmental agencies were created, in part, to serve as a secretariat for one or more cabinet committees. The Federal-Provincial Relations Office in Ottawa, for example, began as a secretariat to the federal government's Cabinet Committee on Federal-Provincial Relations chaired by then Prime Minister Pierre Trudeau. That cabinet committee was disbanded in 1977, although the head of the FPRO maintains the position of "Secretary to the Cabinet for Federal-Provincial Relations".

The Ministry of Intergovernmental Relations (MIR) in British Columbia has responsibility, through a division called the Cabinet Secretariat, for managing and coordinating the operation of the cabinet and all cabinet committees. There are three standing committees, two coordinating committees and three special committees, including one on Federal-Provincial Relations. In addition, the three standing cabinet committees have ancillary committees of deputy ministers. MIR's Cabinet Secretariat serves all of these committees.

In New Brunswick, a Deputy Minister of Intergovernmental Affairs and Legislation advises the Executive Committee of Cabinet on intergovernmental issues. In Prince Edward Island, there is a Cabinet Committee on Intergovernmental Affairs, chaired by the Premier. The Deputy Secretary to Cabinet for Intergovernmental Affairs, the principal official with respect to intergovernmental relations in the province, serves that committee.

Lead Responsibility
All intergovernmental affairs agencies have at one time or another assumed the lead role in some policy areas. Generally, there are four types of policies wherein this function has been performed. These are: constitutional issues; residual policy areas; comprehensive or crossdepartmental policy areas; and "hot" political issues.

Constitutional Issues

During the late 1970s and the early 1980s — the heyday of the constitutional negotiations — all intergovernmental affairs agencies assumed a key role in constitutional matters. There was a multitude of meetings and a large number of documents and proposals generated by governments during this period. Virtually all intergovernmental agencies were expanded. The larger agencies created special "constitutional" units. Even some of the small units in Executive Council Offices bolstered their staffs with constitutional specialists. Delegations to meetings were large because of the scope of the constitutional issue.

Following the proclamation of the Canadian constitution in 1982, events on this front have been relatively quiet. The number of personnel working on constitutional issues has declined and delegations to intergovernmental meetings are smaller. However, it is generally the intergovernmental affairs agencies in all governments that continue to assume responsibility for constitutional issues.

Constitutional matters have not been entirely dormant since 1982. Most important have been the negotiations related to aboriginal matters. As mentioned above, there have been three First Ministers' Conferences (FMCs) to date involving the federal, provincial, and territorial governments, and representatives of the major national aboriginal organizations. Preparation for these conferences has involved numerous meetings at the ministerial and official levels. In addition, four working groups of officials were created at the 1983 FMC; these met several times during the subsequent 12 months.

The role of intergovernmental affairs personnel with respect to aboriginal constitutional issues has varied substantially among the 13 governments sitting at the negotiating table. For example, although the FPRO has not been the only major federal player involved in this area, it has been the principal agency preparing the Prime Minister for the FMCs. As a result, it created a special division in 1983 to handle the aboriginal constitutional matters (Office of Aboriginal Constitutional Affairs). In Ontario, the Ministry of Intergovernmental

Affairs initially took the lead in these matters, but in 1984, this was transferred to an Office of Native Affairs, originally under the Provincial Secretary for Resource Development and subsequently, when that was abolished by Premier David Peterson, under the auspices of the Attorney-General. In Alberta, the Minister of Federal and Intergovernmental Affairs has the lead responsibility on aboriginal constitutional matters, but works closely with the minister responsible for the Native Affairs Secretariat.

Officials in intergovernmental affairs agencies have been called upon from time to time to develop responses to other constitutional issues that arise. Senate reform has been one such recurring issue. When the federal government introduced a resolution in the autumn of 1984 to amend the constitution, changing the Senate's capacity to delay bills, all provincial governments were forced to develop a position. The issue of property rights is another example. A resolution to entrench property rights in the constitution was passed by the British Columbia legislature in 1982. In most governments, it is the intergovernmental affairs agency that develops their position on issues such as these.

Cross-Departmental Issues
Intergovernmental affairs agencies have often assumed responsibility for those issues that involve more than one department. Perhaps the most obvious example of this is regional development policy, which involves policies in virtually every economic sector. In 1974, the federal government signed 10-year bilateral umbrella agreements, known as General Development Agreements (GDAs), with each of the provinces.[21] Subsequently, various subsidiary agreements were signed under the framework of the GDAs. The subsidiary agreements generally covered one sector, such as forestry, fisheries, highways, or a specific region within the province. They provided for a sum of money to be expended by both the federal and the respective provincial governments. When the GDAs expired, new 10-year Economic and Regional Development Agreements (ERDAs) were negotiated to

replace the GDAs. All provinces had signed ERDAs by early 1985.

In several of the provincial governments, the intergovernmental affairs agency has played the key role with respect to these regional development agreements. In Newfoundland, for example, the Intergovernmental Affairs Secretariat (IGS) assumed responsibility for the GDA agreements and the current ERDA agreements. Similarly, in Alberta, that responsibility rests with the Department of Federal and Intergovernmental Affairs (FIGA). In Saskatchewan, the Intergovernmental Affairs Secretariat plays this role. In Manitoba, it is the Clerk of the Executive Council — implicitly the key advisor on intergovernmental affairs — who is responsible for the regional development agreements.

In Nova Scotia, both the GDAs and the ERDAs have been the responsibility of the Department of Development. That department has taken the lead role in the negotiation of these agreements. As such, it acts as Nova Scotia's intergovernmental central agency for economic issues. Similarly, in Prince Edward Island, the Department of Development assumed responsibility for that province's comprehensive agreement until 1981. At that time, the department was disbanded and Intergovernmental Affairs in the Cabinet Office was given responsibility for the regional development agreement. In New Brunswick, it is the secretary to the economic policy cabinet committee who is the chief official for the ERDA agreements.

For the most part, the role of the intergovernmental affairs central agencies — in the governments where they play the coordinating role for the regional development agreements — involves negotiating the umbrella agreement, and defining the term, cost-sharing ratio, and financial commitment of the sectoral subsidiary agreements. Rarely is the intergovernmental agency involved in the actual administration of agreements. The Intergovernmental Affairs Secretariat, for example, administers only one of Newfoundland's subsidiary agreements: the Coastal Labrador agreement. The reason for this lies in the wide variety of sectors affected by the agreement. With respect to Newfoundland's other subsidiary agreements, the relevant sectoral department has assumed the administrative function.

Another issue which tends to cross departmental lines is the Established Programs Financing (EPF) arrangements. These are the federal-provincial fiscal arrangements for the financing of health and post-secondary education programs. Fiscal arrangements, including EPF, are negotiated every five years. The organization of most governments means that three sectoral departments are directly involved: those responsible for health, education, and finance. In many governments, an *ad hoc* interdepartmental committee has been formed to determine the government's position and strategy with respect to EPF negotiations. Officials from the intergovernmental affairs agency usually sit on that committee, and, at times, are part of the negotiating team. However, it is generally recognized in all governments that EPF negotiations are a "finance" issue and, as such, the various finance and treasury departments take the lead in negotiations.

In 1985 and 1986, the issue of free trade negotiations with the United States has become a major issue on the federal-provincial agenda. The nature of the provincial governments' role in Canada's negotiations with the United States remains a key intergovernmental issue. These negotiations will have important implications for most sectors of the economy. As a result, several provincial government departments have a stake in the negotiations. In several governments, the intergovernmental affairs agency is playing an important role, both in coordinating the positions of the line departments and in designing the strategy for dealing with the federal government. *Ad hoc* interdepartmental committees on trade, often chaired by intergovernmental affairs officials, have been established in several governments. This role of the intergovernmental central agency is not new for all agencies. For example, in 1979, responsibility for trade issues fell to FIGA in Alberta. The Deputy Minister of that department chaired an officials' committee on trade issues with respect to the GATT negotiations.

Residual Policy Issues

Intergovernmental agencies have often assumed responsibility for issues for which there is no obvious line department responsible. The constitution could be classified as a special case in this regard. At times, an intergovernmental meeting is convened for a sector in which a government has no department with the necessary policy expertise to handle the relevant issues. As a result, it is often a representative from the central agency who attends. The intergovernmental affairs agency may assume responsibility temporarily, until such time as the issue either disappears or becomes important enough that a separate secretariat or department is formed to handle it.

Examples of such issues include: science and technology (New Brunswick and the Yukon), communications (Newfoundland), and energy (New Brunswick). In Alberta, FIGA assumed responsibility for implementing the Anti-Inflation agreement in 1975.

"Hot" Political Issues

There is no attempt by any intergovernmental affairs agency to be involved in *all* intergovernmental issues. The interface between governments involves a substantial volume of interaction between officials in most line departments. Much of the liaison is very technical and in very narrow fields, and most intergovernmental policy is formulated there. At times, the intergovernmental central agencies get involved in an issue in a rather haphazard fashion. Often, it is only after an issue has reached a stage where it is politically "hot". In such instances, the agency plays essentially a "firefighting" role.

Although all intergovernmental agencies are involved in firefighting to some extent, it is less prevalent in departments that have a comprehensive monitoring system in place, where most hot issues can be anticipated before they reach the political crisis stage. An examination of the evolution of the Ministry of Intergovernmental Affairs in Ontario illustrates that firefighting was more prevalent in the earlier years of the department, until a policy development unit was established.

If an issue is perceived to have broad significance, affecting the "corporate image" of the government, then it is often inevitable that the intergovernmental unit will be involved, either assisting the relevant sectoral department, or perhaps even taking over responsibility. The debate over the *Canada Health Act* in 1983 provides an example.[22] The introduction of that bill was perceived by most provinces to be more than just a health department issue: it was seen as a major federal initiative in an area of provincial jurisdiction. As such, the intergovernmental affairs specialists in most provinces played an important role in determining their government's response and strategy.

A related role occasionally performed by intergovernmental affairs officials may be termed "mediating." Impasses between line departments of two governments have often been resolved by negotiations between the two intergovernmental affairs agencies.

International Relations

One area of responsibility that recently has assumed a greater prominence in several of the provincial intergovernmental affairs departments — notably those in Ontario, Alberta, and, until 1984, Quebec — is international relations. The enhancement of trading opportunities is the principal reason for the provincial foray into the international arena. There are essentially three functions which intergovernmental affairs agencies perform with respect to international affairs. These are: the overall coordination of a government's international relations; the administration of external offices; and protocol duties.

Coordination of Government's International Activities

The agencies for intergovernmental affairs in several of the provinces assume responsibility for the province's international matters. Such functions include: coordinating interaction between provincial departments and agencies and other countries; monitoring events and briefing provincial officials on developments in other nations; and handling various social and cultural aspects of a province's interaction with foreign countries. The nature of provincial-international relations is such that it is essential that the provincial officials, usually in the intergovernmental affairs agencies, work closely with officials in the federal Department of External Affairs.

International relations have always had a special significance in Quebec. Not only interested in enhancing its trading opportunities, Quebec has also been actively engaged in promoting itself as a part of the French-speaking world, seeking to be represented itself, rather than by the federal government, in conferences involving francophone nations. From the early 1970s until 1984, Quebec's international relations were an integral part of its *Ministère des affaires intergouvernementales*. In 1984, a reorganization put international affairs in a department of its own. Since the election of the Liberal government in December 1985, both report to the same minister.

Administration of External Offices (International)
Some provinces administer offices located in other countries. For the most part, these are primarily geared towards the enhancement of trade and economic relations. Quebec has a special relationship with other French-speaking nations — several of its offices serve primarily cultural purposes.

Although several provincial foreign offices are administered by the intergovernmental affairs agencies, in some provinces, foreign offices are administered by the department responsible for trade relations. In Ontario, although three offices are administered by the Ministry of Intergovernmental Affairs (Brussels, Paris and Frankfurt), most foreign offices are the responsibility of the Ministry of Industry, Trade and Tourism. Similarly, in Alberta, certain international offices are administered by the Department of Federal and Intergovernmental Affairs (Tokyo, New York, London and Hong Kong), while others are under the responsibility of the Economic Development Department. In Quebec, since 1984, all international offices are the responsibility of the *Ministère des relations internationales*.

Protocol Functions
Most provincial and territorial intergovernmental affairs agencies have responsibility for protocol duties. Such duties include briefing visiting dignitaries from other countries, as well as handling the arrangements and logistics of such visits. Officials in these agencies also make arrangements and brief premiers, ministers and their staff prior to official visits to other nations.

POWER

Degrees of Power
Intergovernmental affairs agencies vary substantially in the amount of power they wield. A central agency's power is measured primarily in terms of its influence on the policy-making process. Donald Wallace suggests a continuum of levels of coordination. Levels range from "monitoring" or "supervision" through "advisory", "service" and "policy coordination" to the more substantive "control".[23] Some intergovernmental affairs agencies exert a substantial amount of control over the sectoral departments, while others assume no more than an advisory role. For these agencies, the extent to which they have any influence depends on how much the sectoral departments choose to listen.

Exercise of Power
The above summary of functions has illustrated some ways in which intergovernmental affairs agencies exercise power. Included are the signing of agreements and the monitoring of submissions to cabinet. These are not the only levers of power which an intergovernmental affairs agency can have. For example, in Quebec, at one time, all out-of-province travel by provincial government officials, except for that to the national capital region, had to be approved by the *Ministère des Affaires intergouvernementales.*

Intergovernmental affairs agencies can hold power as a result of the unique position that they occupy in a government. From their perspective as "overseers" and coordinators, intergovernmental officials may be aware of developments in all policy sectors, both within their own government and within other governments. This latter capacity to obtain information on the perceptions and positions of other governments enables intergovernmental officials to influence the policy process.[24]

One problem with trying to measure the influence of an agency is that it is often difficult to separate the influence that is personal from the influence than is attributable to an institution. The nature of a central agency's influence is often the result of a central agency official's efforts, personality, interest and drive.[25]

Sources of Power

There are various sources from which an intergovernmental agency may obtain its power. One is the legislative authority to exercise certain measures of control. Most often, this is a statutory provision wherein the signature of the minister responsible for intergovernmental affairs is required before an agreement with another government is valid. In departments of intergovernmental affairs that have such powers guaranteed in legislation, such as Quebec, Alberta and Newfoundland, officials and ministers from intergovernmental affairs agencies are usually included in the initial stages of negotiations. Some statutes which created intergovernmental departments forbid sectoral department officials or ministers from stating official government positions in negotiations with other governments without the authorization from the minister responsible for intergovernmental affairs.

While potentially a significant source of power, statutory provisions are by no means complete. It is conceivable that a line department which objects to the measure of central control imposed by the statute, can keep the central agency, at least to some extent, "in the dark". Intergovernmental interaction involves more than negotiating agreements. The central agency is largely at the mercy of the line departments with respect to the amount of information it receives and when it receives it.

It is important to note the distinction between what has been termed here the "exercise" of power and the "sources" of power. Having a statutory hammer does not necessarily mean that an agency exercises real power. Conversely, not having a statutory grant of authority does not mean that an agency does not exercise comparable power. Essentially, intergovernmental agencies acquire an element of power to the extent that they receive timely and consistent information with respect to intergovernmental relations, and to the extent that they have the capacity to have an impact on policy formulation. Their power is a combination of information and influence.

A second source of power is the backing of the first minister or other senior minister. Administrative policy can be as strong as statutory power if it is supported by the first minister. Such policy can ensure that all intergovernmental agreements are co-signed by the intergovernmental affairs ministers, that the agency be consulted before any interaction with other governments is taken, and that all correspondence with other governments be sent to the agency.

In Ontario, for example, in August 1985, Premier David Peterson sent to all ministers and deputy ministers, a letter outlining the services which the Ministry of Intergovernmental Affairs (MIA) provides. It listed various instances where the sectoral departments were advised to contact the MIA. Similarily, in Alberta, in the early 1970s, two memos were sent by Peter Lougheed. One stated that a copy of all correspondence with other governments was to be sent to the Department of Federal and Intergovernmental Affairs (FIGA). The other stated that a FIGA official had to be at all intergovernmental ministerial meetings. Concerning the federal government, Richard Van Loon, writing during the last year of the Trudeau government, predicted that if the FPRO retained "strong leadership and staff and, most importantly, the trust of the Prime Minister, [it would] remain a significant force in determining how Ottawa decides."[26]

A third source of power is expertise and a good track record. Some intergovernmental affairs units are consulted by the sectoral departments because their input is valued. Initially, central agencies have been regarded with some suspicion. Some, however, have been able, over time, to develop a source of power based on their record. This source of power may be more tenuous than the others — a conflict of objectives or strategies between a department and the intergovernmental affairs agency could render the latter impotent. It has been suggested, for example, that although FIGA in Alberta, has significant legislatively-based powers, including signing authority over all intergovernmental agreements, any success that it has enjoyed has depended more on the ability of its officials to maintain credibility and trust. To achieve its goals, FIGA has relied heavily on the force of personality, not trying to take over anyone else's responsibilities, providing very good advice, maintaining a dialogue with other departments and not proceeding in a heavy-handed manner.[27]

Some intergovernmental agencies have an additional source of power as a result of their proximity to the first minister. An intergovernmental affairs unit in the Executive Council Office of a government may be better able to discipline a line department than a separate department of intergovernmental affairs. The former has the implicit backing of the premier or prime minister.

In the past two years, there has been a tendency to locate intergovernmental relations units at the centre of power. Currently, the intergovernmental units in the federal government and in the Governments of Manitoba, Saskatchewan, Quebec, Prince Edward Island, New Brunswick, Newfoundland and the Yukon are situated in the Executive Council Office or First Ministers' Office. Moreover, in most governments, it is the first minister who currently assumes responsibility for relations with other governments. This is the case in Saskatchewan, Manitoba, Ontario, New Brunswick, Nova Scotia, Prince Edward Island, and the Northwest and Yukon Territories. Federally, Prime Minister Brian Mulroney speaks for the Government of Canada in all federal-provincial matters.

Proximity to the premier is not always a source of power, however. The predecessor to the Department of Federal and Intergovernmental Affairs (FIGA) in Alberta was a small unit in the Executive Council Office. According to Donald Getty, the first Minister of FIGA, that agency was mostly ignored by the line departments "because the conditions, the co-ordination and the policy control was just non-existent....[It] did not have the proper support."[28] In Alberta, it was felt that power could best be exercised by a separate department. The Executive Council Office is not a strong central agency in the Alberta government. This is the reverse of the situation in other provinces, where an agency can accrue power simply from being in the Executive Council Office.

This example highlights the differences in political cultures and circumstances within various governments. It serves as a warning that what is a source of power in one government may not be a source of power in another.

Notes

1. R.M. Burns, *Intergovernmental Liaison on Fiscal and Economic Matters*. Kingston: Institute of Intergovernmental Relations, 1968, pp. 290-1.
2. Donald V. Smiley, *Constitutional Adaptation and Canadian Federalism Since 1945*. Document of the Royal Commission on Bilingualism and Biculturalism, no. 4. Ottawa:Information Canada, 1970, p. 111.
3. Howard Leeson, "Accommodative Mechanisms in a Decentralizing Federation: The Intergovernmental Affairs Function in Saskatchewan." Presented to the Institute for Public Administration, St. John's, 30 August 1985, p. 20.
4. Kenneth Kernaghan, "Intergovernmental Administrative Relations in Canada." in K. Kernaghan, ed. *Public Administration in Canada, Selected Readings, 4th ed.*, Toronto: Methuen, 1982, p. 84.
5. Timothy Woolstencroft, "Intergovernmental Emissaries - The Provincial Guardians of the Federal Bargain: A Case Study of Alberta and Ontario," (unpublished M.A. thesis, Queen's University), 1980, p. 135.
6. Ian D. Clark. "Recent Changes in the Cabinet Decision-making System in Ottawa." *Canadian Public Administration*, 28:2, 1985, p. 200.
7. Woolstencroft, p. 238.

8. Don Stevenson, "The Role of Intergovernmental Conferences in the Decision-making Process." in R. Simeon, ed. *Confrontation and Collaboration - Intergovernmental Relations in Canada Today.* Toronto: The Institute of Public Administration of Canada, 1979, p. 98.

9. Government of Alberta. Department of Federal and Intergovernmental Affairs, *Tenth Annual Report,* 1984, p. 9.

10. Donald Savoie, "The Continuing Struggle for a Regional Development Policy" in P.M. Leslie, ed. *Canada: The State of the Federation, 1985,* Kingston: Institute of Intergovernmental Relations, 1985, p. 141.

11. P. Aucoin and H. Bakvis, "Regional Responsiveness and Government Organization: The Case of Regional Economic Development Policy in Canada." in P. Aucoin, ed. *Regional Responsiveness and the National Administrative State.* Toronto: University of Toronto Press (Volume 37, Royal Commission on the Economic Union and Development Prospects for Canada research study), 1985, p. 109.

12. Aucoin and Bakvis, p. 111.

13. Burns, p. 291.

14. Interview.

15. Government of Saskatchewan. *Debates and Proceedings,* Vol. 26, 20 April 1983, p. 1259.

16. J. P. Meekison, "First Ministers' Conferences in the Canadian Federal System." in T. Courchene et al, ed. *Ottawa and the Provinces: The Distribution of Money and Power. Volume 2.* Toronto: Ontario Economic Council, 1985, p. 164.

17. There was no Western Premiers' Conference in 1982 (because the host province, Saskatchewan, had an election and there was a change of government). Also, there was no conference held in 1975.

18. Audrey Doerr, *The Machinery of Government in Canada.* Toronto: Methuen, 1981, p. 33 .

19. Government of Canada. *House of Commons Debates,* 18 December 1974, p. 2374.

20. Donald C. Wallace, "Provincial Central Agencies for Intergovernmental Relations and the Policy Process."

(unpublished Ph.D dissertation, York University), 1985, p. 362.
21. Except for Prince Edward Island, which reached a long-term Comprehensive Development Plan in 1969. It was divided into three phases, the final going into effect in 1980.
22. See D. Hawkes and B. Pollard, "The Medicare Debate in Canada: The Politics of the New Federalism." *Publius. The Journal of Federalism,* Vol. 14:3, 1984, pp. 183-98.
23. Wallace, p. 29.
24. K. Kernaghan, "The Power and Responsibility of Intergovernmental Officials in Canada." Prepared for the Annual Conference of the Institute of Public Administration of Canada, Winnipeg, 31 August 1979, p. 10.
25. Gordon Robertson, quoted in Donald Wallace, p. 366.
26. R. Van Loon, "Planning in the Eighties." in French and Van Loon, *How Ottawa Decides, Second Edition,* Toronto: Lorimer and Co., 1984, p. 177.
27. Wallace, p. 33.
28. Government of Alberta. *Alberta Hansard,* 10 March 1972, p. 7-25.

3 EXPLAINING THE VARIETY

The rise of intergovernmental affairs agencies has not been uniform across the country. While all governments have seen the need for some such unit or department, two of the most notable features of intergovernmental affairs agencies in Canada have been the great variety which exists among them, and the propensity for change within them. This chapter focuses on what factors influence the structures that governments establish to handle intergovernmental relations.

Underlying this discussion is the assumption that there is a direct relationship between bureaucratic organization and forces within society. The 1963 report of the Royal Commission on Government Organization (Glassco Commission) observed that "the organization of government, no less than the policies it pursues, must reflect the order of importance, in the minds of the public, of the problems requiring attention."[1] Aucoin and Bakvis note that:

> while governmental organization is a determinant of national policy, albeit only one among many, it is also the subject of government policy. It is so precisely because the manner in which the government is organized affects the distribution of authority, power and influence in ways that are

not politically or policy neutral. A particular organizational structure will give certain ideas and interests an edge over competing ideas and interests by virtue of the way it distributes authority, power and influence within the cabinet and bureaucracy.[2]

Explaining the Variety

Several factors can account for the variation among intergovernmental affairs agencies with respect to their structures, functions, powers, and resources. Howard Leeson writes: "The need to develop bureaucratic mechanisms to accommodate increased intergovernmental activity, and the type of agency developed, obviously vary depending on the social, economic and political context."[3] Following is a summary of some of the factors that help to explain the variety among the agencies.

Population Size and Fiscal Strength

The form of bureaucratic organization adopted by a government is strongly influenced by the size of the government and its fiscal strength. The effect on intergovernmental affairs agencies can be felt in several ways. For example, a small government may not need a central agency to coordinate its intergovernmental affairs to the same extent as a larger government. Coordination may be less difficult for a small government. Governments in Prince Edward Island, New Brunswick, Manitoba, and Nova Scotia have found that small units in the Executive Council Office, often comprising only one or two professional staff, are sufficient to ensure the degree of coordination that these governments feel is necessary.

The size of the government is a factor in determining the capacity of the Federal-Provincial Relations Office (FPRO) to coordinate policy at the federal level. Roger Gibbins observes that "the conduct of federal-provincial relations can be centralized to only a limited degree.... With a staff of approximately sixty officials, FPRO cannot *direct* the conduct of federal-provincial relations across the massive federal bureaucracy."[4]

Donald Savoie notes that the fiscal capacity of a provincial government has a profound impact on how the government approaches federal-provincial relations.[5] He suggests that a poor province may not always be able to pull together the necessary expertise to contribute fully to the intergovernmental policy and program formulation process. Similarly, Van Loon and Whittington suggest that the "rationalist" processes which were implemented in most of the larger governments during the 1960s and 1970s have affected the way federal-provincial bargaining takes place. The ability to bargain effectively has, in part, become linked to whether a government's policy priorities are articulated in rationalist terms. Governments lacking the necessary manpower resources may be "functionally disfranchised" from taking a full part in federal-provincial interaction.[6] As well, a government with a weak fiscal position may be forced to discard initiatives it favours for others of lower priority, but which are eligible for federal cost-sharing.

A province's fiscal capacity can affect the number of resources that a government is able to devote exclusively to intergovernmental relations. Michael Jenkin's examination of the Canadian Council of Resource and Environment Ministers (CCREM) reveals that many of the smaller governments became dissatisfied with the substantial drain on the resources of their officials that was required by that intergovernmental body.[7]

Philosophy of the Government
Among the most important factors that account for the particular shape that organization within governments takes is the position or philosophy of the government. Theoretically, the government embodies the will of the electorate. The views and wishes of the people can be reflected in both the organization and the policies that are developed. Government positions and views on the following issues can affect how a government organizes its intergovernmental relations:

1. general philosophical approach
2. intergovernmental objectives

3. approach to federal-provincial relations
4. position on specific issues
5. personal goals

1. General Philosophical Approach
There are several interrelated elements in a government's general philosophical approach. Whether it is more inclined to be activist, rather than non-interventionist and oriented towards *laissez-faire* policies, will affect a government's views on central agencies, strategic planning, and the size of government generally. These views will have direct implications for how the government approaches and organizes its intergovernmental relations.

The philosophical leaning of a government can help to explain quite different approaches and styles of organization adopted by governments in provinces having similar sizes of population. Saskatchewan, Nova Scotia, New Brunswick and Newfoundland have similar population sizes, yet very different types of intergovernmental affairs agencies.

Some governments have advocated smaller government as a goal in itself. For these, it is important that the number and size of agencies and departments be kept to a minimum. Sterling Lyon, for example, assumed power in Manitoba in 1980 on a platform that promised, among other things, less government. During his term, intergovernmental relations were essentially the work of one individual in the Executive Council Office. Although Sterling Lyon's Progressive Conservative government was replaced in 1982, the subsequent New Democratic government appears to be equally cautious about increasing the size of government. Although an intergovernmental affairs secretariat was created in the Executive Council Office in 1984, it is very small and the government appears to be wary of an increase in size.

Related to a government's view on the size of government is its attitude towards central agencies, including intergovernmental affairs units. The Lyon government in Manitoba held "ministerial responsibility" as an ideal and, as such, it was suspicious of central agencies generally. Line departments were responsible for intergovernmental affairs policy and, for that matter, virtually all policy. The coordination of relations with other governments did not exist in any systematic or comprehensive way.

Another aspect of a government's general philosophical approach is its view on "rationalization" within governments. According to Donald Smiley, rationalization involves three imperatives:

- the objectives and priorities of public policy should be explicitly stated;
- the aims of policy should be stated at a higher level of generality and more specific aims controlled by broader ones;
- the effectiveness and efficiency of all programs should be evaluated. [8]

While the extent to which a government embraces these ideals is, in part, a product of the general philosophical stance of the particular government in power, it is also a reflection of the times. The late 1960s and early 1970s was the period of the "rationalization" movement in governments. It began in the United States and was manifested in a variety of forms: Planning, Programming, Budgeting System (PPBS), Zero-based Budgeting (ZBB), and Management by Objectives (MBO), for example. Donald Wallace suggests that one reason for the Alberta Department of Federal and Intergovernmental Affairs' extensive coordinating power lies in the fact that the department was created during the early 1970s, a period of intense government expansion in the country, especially with respect to coordinating mechanisms and central agencies. [9] Efforts towards rationalization were also consistent with Premier Lougheed's technocratic bent. However, the Ministry of Intergovernmental Affairs in Ontario was established in 1978, by which time the role and power of central mechanisms was being seriously questioned.

One impact of the rationalization schemes implemented by both federal and provincial governments is that horizontal relationships between officials were weakened when, especially in areas of broad policy, provincial premiers and other central officials began to use hierarchical controls to exert greater dominance over program departments.[10] This had important implications for the organization of intergovernmental relations. The centralization of power diminished the independence of specialist relationships between operating departments at the expense of central agencies. The creation of common policies for all federal-provincial relationships within a government became an objective in itself. The establishment of intergovernmental affairs central agencies was thus consistent with the move towards rationalization in governments.

2. Intergovernmental Objectives

There seems to be a strong correlation between a government's intergovernmental objectives – what it hopes to attain from its interaction with other governments – and the power and structure of its intergovernmental affairs agency. During the 1960s, with a lead role played by Quebec, several provincial governments developed strong objectives in the intergovernmental realm. These included the pursuit of an expanded provincial jurisdiction, the rollback of federal intrusions, and greater fiscal autonomy. Many became "more sensitive to jurisdictional issues, more alert to federal encroachments onto their constitutional turf" than they had been previously.[11] The creation of separate intergovernmental affairs agencies was one effect of these more ambitious intergovernmental objectives.

There seem to be two aspects to the relationship between such objectives and the establishment of powerful central agencies for coordinating relations with other governments. First, an intergovernmental affairs unit can provide a government with ammunition or the necessary expertise to enable it to stand up to the other level, to do battle, or to bargain from a position of strength. A large intergovernmental affairs bureaucracy provides the necessary support for a government either defending itself against intrusions or "on the attack". This support includes statistical and other evidence, legal opinions on various issues that are causing friction, and information on a vast array of policy sectors wherein a government can argue that the other level of government is infringing. An intergovernmental agency can provide examples of past injustices, and generally help a government to argue its case from an informed position. In order to be able to withstand the centralizing pull of a strong federal government, it is important that a province have a strong position, supported by rational argumentation.

A second aspect of the relationship between the type of intergovernmental affairs agency and a government's intergovernmental objectives is that in a period of conflict, the management of the total picture is perceived to be more important. It is more crucial that a government have a single position *vis à vis* the other order of government. It is essential that all departments toe the government line — and not make deals on their own.

Governments worried about line departments reaching intergovernmental agreements that may not be best for the government as a whole, that may distort the spending priorities of the government, or that may be contrary to the government's overall philosophy or objectives, might feel a special need to have a strong central coordinating body. It is argued that all interaction with the "other side" should be monitored and approved by a single agency which is close to the first minister. Tight control and coordination by an intergovernmental affairs unit are essential for a government that is fighting for its jurisdiction.

There are differing opinions about why some governments have pursued these vigorous intergovernmental objectives. Three different explanations can be summarized. First, Timothy Woolstencroft argues that the differences in the power and prestige of the intergovernmental affairs agencies are largely a reflection of two factors: the intensity of dissatisfaction with Canadian federalism, and the strength of the other central agencies within the government.[12] The second of these will be addressed later. With respect to the first, Woolstencroft asserts that some governments have created powerful coordinating agencies because they are disenchanted with the federal system and the behaviour of the federal government. Others have created less powerful advisory agencies because they are more content with the federal system and less worried by the implications of Ottawa's policy thrusts.

Implicit in this argument is the notion that there may be a symbolic message in the way in which a government organizes itself. A government with an intergovernmental agency imbued with substantial powers is often perceived to be defending its jurisdiction against intrusions from the other level of government. If not an outright declaration of war, it is a signal that it is prepared to do battle in order to defend what it considers to be its jurisdiction, thereby challenging the claims of the other.

Conversely, some governments have chosen not to create a large intergovernmental affairs department imbued with substantial powers precisely because they do not hold such a view. Governments such as New Brunswick and Manitoba have opted for a more "low-key" approach to intergovernmental relations. This is consistent with the "niche" in Confederation which these provinces have traditionally filled.

Canadian federalism can be seen as a constant struggle between centralist and decentralist tendencies. A province that feels the federal government is too strong and the pendulum is swinging too much towards the centralist direction, or a federal government that feels the country is becoming too decentralist, is more likely to create a strong and powerful intergovernmental affairs agency.

A second perspective is offered by Donald Wallace who disagrees with explaining the differences in power and prestige among the various intergovernmental affairs agencies in terms of intensity of satisfaction or dissatisfaction with the federation. Wallace sees the development of these agencies as a natural evolution flowing from the change in thought that took place in some governments during the 1960s.[13] For provinces that have historically been predisposed ideologically towards the decentralization of the federation — such as Quebec, Alberta, and Newfoundland — there was a natural inclination to set up a coordinating agency with special responsibilities for the constitution.

The creation of intergovernmental affairs departments in these governments was largely motivated by ideological concerns. According to Wallace's argument, these governments saw the necessity of strengthening their ability to understand the federal government and to negotiate with it on equal terms. In 1971, Premier Lougheed of Alberta, for example, inherited a staff lacking a sophisticated understanding of the federal government and the intergovernmental relations system. The Department of Federal and Intergovernmental Affairs (FIGA) was created largely to fill that void. Wallace asserts that it is "quite a different matter" to contend, as Timothy Woolstencroft has done, that the power and prestige of central agencies for intergovernmental affairs are a reflection of that province's intensity of dissatisfaction with Canadian federalism.[14]

Furthermore, a provincial or territorial government that perceives itself to be on the periphery of Canadian federalism – regarded as an outpost by the federal government – may feel that it has to present its case more strongly than others. This could result in the creation of a strong and powerful agency. A key reason for the creation of FIGA in Alberta was to enable Alberta to be "an equal partner in Confederation".[15]

Third, Donald Smiley asserts that ascendent provincial elites in Alberta and Quebec were dissatisfied with Canadian federalism and, as such, directly challenged the powers of the federal government.[16] Because of the importance of intergovernmental activities to the objectives of the elites that dominate these two governments, the intergovernmental affairs departments have substantial staff resources and political strength. They are able to control the external relations of sectoral departments in the interest of jurisdiction-wide objectives. At the federal level, the Federal-Provincial Relations Office has been partly motivated to sustain and enhance federal power, particularly when this power and the continuing existence of Confederation itself are under attack.[17]

3. Approach to Federal-Provincial Relations

A government's approach to federal-provincial relations can have an impact on the structure and powers of its intergovernmental affairs agency. An example is provided by the "new federalism" approach of the federal government during the early 1980s. Grounded in a belief that the forces of decentralization had become too strong during the previous decade, this approach emphasized national standards, visibility and direct delivery of programs by the federal government. Marked by unilateral action and a lack of cooperation, this approach led to a low point in federal-provincial relations and to much acrimony between the orders of government.

The new federalism had a mixed effect on the power of intergovernmental affairs agencies. On one hand, the decline in consultation and the reduction in the volume of first ministers' and other ministers' meetings that accompanied the "new federalism" signalled less need for a large intergovernmental bureaucracy. On the other hand, because this period was marked by tension and conflict, for governments that adopted a "battle mentality", a strong support agency was needed.

In the current Canadian situation, there exists a belief among governments that it is preferable to work together, and this was the message that came from the Canadian electorate on 4 September 1984. Canadians want the federal and provincial governments to cooperate. That message not only registered on the new federal government, which had made intergovernmental cooperation a key plank in its electoral platform, but also on the politicians and officials in the provincial governments.

Public expectations can be important in determining how a government approaches its intergovernmental relations and, indirectly, how a government organizes to fulfill these expectations. In trying to explain the differences between the intergovernmental affairs departments in Alberta and Ontario, Timothy Woolstencroft argues that it is politically less expedient for an Ontario government to be strongly opposed to the federal government than it is for an Alberta government to criticize Ottawa.[18]

Accepting that interdependence in virtually every policy area is inevitable, an approach to intergovernmental affairs that emphasizes cooperation and collaboration appears to be the objective of all governments during the early years of the Mulroney government. It is generally accepted that "a truly effective national policy can only come about when the two orders of government co-ordinate their programs and policies across a broad range of areas, all of which are interdependent and all of which contribute to national policy. [Therefore,] the effective co-ordination of government activities requires that there be agreement to work in a common direction."[19]

However, the Report of the Royal Commission on the Economic Union and Development Prospects for Canada notes that "shared purposes alone are not enough to establish positive relationships: they need to be supported by effective consultation and debate if co-ordinated results are to emerge."[20] As a result, the influence of intergovernmental affairs agencies, with their expertise in interacting and negotiating with other governments, may increase in a period when governments are motivated to cooperate.

A government's approach to federal-provincial relations may influence a first minister's choice concerning the appointment of a minister responsible for intergovernmental affairs. A strong minister may be better able to defend his province's jurisdiction in multilateral sessions. Moreover, a government's approach may have an impact on the decision to create a separate department of intergovernmental affairs as opposed to a branch in the Executive Council Office. A government that is keen to adopt a "hardline" with other governments might be more inclined to have a separate department and minister handle this role. In this fashion, the premier is not so closely linked to tough and perhaps conflictual negotiations. It has been suggested that the 1972 appointment of Donald Getty as the first Minister of Intergovernmental Affairs in Alberta by then Premier Peter Lougheed enabled the province to use a "good cop-bad cop" routine in negotiations with Ottawa. "Getty, the bad cop, would open negotiations with a tough uncompromising stance. Then Lougheed, playing good cop, would take over, bending a little and bargaining a lot."[21]

4. Position on Specific Issues

The specific objectives of a government with respect to a given issue can affect how it organizes itself. For example, a government may wish to emphasize a particular sector or issue by creating a separate department or agency.

Governments that have a single "burning issue" or that tend to be primarily driven by one sector, are more likely to have a strong, coordinated approach to their relations with the other level of government. For example, during the last few years of the Trudeau regime, it was important for the Governments of Alberta and Newfoundland to generally have single positions *vis à vis* Ottawa, regardless of the policy area. Because much of Alberta's economy is structured on the oil industry, policy in that sector is crucial to the government. The position of the federal government with respect to energy policy colours Alberta's relations with Ottawa in virtually all sectors.

Similarly, for years, the Government of Newfoundland pinned the provinces' economic future on offshore resources. As long as the federal government held a position which would not give the province control over the development of these resources, the tone of all of Newfoundland's interaction with Ottawa was acrimonious. Coordination of all interaction was crucial in order to ensure that a single provincial position on intergovernmental relations was maintained. After the Mulroney government promised to give Newfoundland an equal say in the management of the offshore, relations with the federal government became positive in *all* sectors.

The nature of the Ontario economy makes the adoption of such an approach there less likely. Officials in the Ontario government argue that because of the complex and diverse economic base of the province, it is impossible for the government to adopt a single approach to intergovernmental relations. For political reasons, the

Ontario government cannot be driven by one issue or sector. For Ontario, it is perfectly acceptable to be in total agreement with the federal government on one issue and, at the same time, to oppose federal policy in another area.

5. Personal Goals

The personality and goals of key political actors can also be important. Donald Smiley has noted that under Prime Minister Trudeau, there was a rapid development in machinery for dealing with federal-provincial relations (most notably, the creation of a cabinet committee and the Federal-Provincial Relations Office in the Privy Council Office). This was, in part, a reflection of Mr. Trudeau's preoccupation with questions relating to federalism, and in part, his aggressive concern with rationalizing the operations of government.[22] Campbell and Szablowski note that the philosophical approach of Pierre Trudeau in 1968 combined an intense commitment to rationality with the pursuit of functional, pragmatic politics.[23]

Similarly, the personal interest of some first ministers in intergovernmental affairs can have implications for the structure. For example, Premier Richard Hatfield of New Brunswick places a high level of importance on negotiations and discussions — and personal interaction — among first ministers, and less on briefing books and strategic planning. This has been a factor in keeping New Brunswick's intergovernmental bureaucracy to a minimum.

Bureaucratic Organization

The nature and power of the intergovernmental affairs agency in some governments may be partly explained by bureaucratic pressure and structure. Timothy Woolstencroft asserts that the presence of other central agencies inhibits the development of a strong intergovernmental affairs agency.[24] As a result, such an agency usually has less power within a government. In Saskatchewan, for example, a strong Department of Finance was able to ensure that an intergovernmental affairs department with powers similar to those exercised by the Department of Federal and Intergovernmental Affairs in Alberta did not emerge in Regina.[25] In the Yukon government, jealous line departments helped make the Department of Intergovernmental Relations quite powerless. That department was subsequently made a part of the Executive Council Office. Similarly, Nova Scotia's Office of Intergovernmental Affairs, inaugurated in 1979, never assumed the real powers of a central agency primarily because of uncooperative line departments. It lacked both a statutory base and the firm support of the Premier.

At the federal level, VanLoon and Whittington have observed that the FPRO has never been able to gain the broad coordinative clout of other central agencies.[26] Its primary functions have been of a monitoring and surveillance nature. Moreover, it is suggested that because of the attitudes in other central agencies and in key line departments, any attempt to increase its role to coordinator of federal activities in the intergovernmental arena would be opposed quite vigorously.

Explaining the Changes

There have been several changes in the structural arrangements of intergovernmental affairs agencies in recent years. These have included the creation and the disbanding of agencies, as well as organizational changes within them. The following discussion summarizes some of the more important factors that cause changes in the structures, functions and powers of intergovernmental affairs agencies.

A cautionary note must be inserted here. Not all structural changes reflect an underlying change in direction or approach. Often, they are simply the result of a new minister's or premier's particular preference or idiosyncracy. Or they may reflect a change in personnel at the officials level.

Economic Conditions

The way in which governments organize can reflect, in part, economic and social conditions. The decline in size, or the outright elimination of an agency or department can be part of a general restraint program, the consequence of a government bent on curbing spending. The decline in resources allocated to intergovernmental units in recent years in some jurisdictions may reflect, in part, efforts by all governments to enact policies of restraint. It can be argued that agencies such as intergovernmental affairs units are among the easiest — politically — to cut during a period of restraint because they neither administer any programs of their own nor have any client group.

Issues on the Agenda
It has already been noted that the presence of numerous intergovernmental and cross-departmental issues on the public agenda was a factor in the creation of intergovernmental affairs agencies in most governments in Canada. Beyond that, the particular mix of issues on the intergovernmental agenda at any one time can affect the way in which intergovernmental affairs agencies themselves are organized.

The prevalence of the constitution on the agenda during the late 1970s meant that most intergovernmental departments had a constitutional branch. Apart from simply affecting the organizational situation within intergovernmental affairs agencies, a second consequence of the constitutional debates was that the policy coordination activities of many of these agencies received less emphasis. For example, during the first effort to reform the constitution (1968 to 1971), Ontario's small Federal-Provincial and Interprovincial Secretariat tended to focus on the constitutional issue "to the detriment of its other functions, such as the day-to-day monitoring and coordinating of the intergovernmental activities of the program ministries."[27]

After the patriation of the constitution in 1982, several organizational changes were made to the Federal-Provincial Relations Office (FPRO) in Ottawa, reflecting a changed public agenda. The Office of Aboriginal Constitutional Affairs was created as part of FPRO in 1983, in response to the fact that constitutional matters as they related to Canada's aboriginal peoples would be on the agenda at least until 1987. As well, social and economic policy secretariats were created and a large proportion of FPRO's resources channelled into these, reflecting the increased importance of these issues on the intergovernmental agenda.

It was noted in Chapter Two that intergovernmental affairs agencies often assume responsibility for issues which are "cross-departmental" in nature, or do not fall within the purview of existing departments. As such, when there are several such issues on the public agenda, the central agency for intergovernmental relations often assumes a greater importance. Conversely, as Donald Wallace notes, when most intergovernmental issues involve one line ministry negotiating solely with its counterpart in another government, any role which the intergovernmental agency may play is likely to be simply of an advisory nature.[28]

Interaction With Other Governments

The way in which governments organize their intergovernmental affairs may be affected by the nature of their interaction with other governments. Two factors that can affect organization are the volume of interaction and the structures adopted by other governments.

1. The Volume of Interaction

Generally the greater the amount of interaction among governments, the greater the number of meetings that must be attended. As a result, there is more need for "process" experts – specialists at negotiating, interacting and developing "meeting strategy". Often, officials with this expertise are in the intergovernmental affairs agencies.

The number of intergovernmental meetings has increased dramatically since the postwar years. Richard Simeon noted that between 1967 and 1977, the annual number of intergovernmental ministerial and officials meetings more than doubled.[29] During the ensuing years and because of the drive towards the patriation of the constitution (1978-81), there was an even greater volume of intergovernmental meetings. Federal-provincial relations was a growth industry, with the airlines, hotels and restaurants across the country being major benefactors. Following that hectic period, the degree of formal interaction decreased and the size of delegations to meetings was scaled down. This was due both to the decline in importance of constitutional issues on the public agenda, and to the effects of the recession which pervaded the Canadian economy in 1982 and 1983.

Since the federal election of 4 September 1984, the number of federal-provincial meetings has again increased dramatically. The return to an "era of cooperation" has led to a substantial increase in the volume of interaction. In the first 12 months after the election of the Mulroney government, there were 438 meetings of first ministers, ministers, or deputy ministers involving the federal government and at least one provincial government.[30]

One effect of the increase in the number of meetings during the late 1970s was the appointment of a separate minister in some governments to handle the constitutional portfolio on behalf of the first minister. Many first ministers considered it impossible to attend all ministerial meetings on the constitution. This was an important reason lying behind the creation of a Department of Intergovernmental Affairs in Saskatchewan and the appointment of a senior minister to head the department. In Ontario, the separation of Intergovernmental Affairs from the Treasury came in part from the need for a "front man" to participate in the constitutional debate on behalf of the Premier. It was acknowledged that the Treasury was already burdened with a large number of "finance" issues. In some governments, other ministers, such as the Minister of Justice or the Attorney-General, assumed the key role on the constitution.

The other side of this argument is that since 1982, there has not been the same need for a separate minister of intergovernmental affairs. It is no longer a "full-time" position. This argument has been used to explain the recent tendency for first ministers to assume responsibility in this area. However, a recognition of the importance of intergovernmental issues seems to be a larger factor in explaining this trend.

A second impact of the increased interaction with other governments on intergovernmental agencies relates to their role as support staff to the first minister. The more conferences involving the first minister, the greater the demands on the intergovernmental affairs agency. In the fourteen months following the election of the Mulroney government, there were three full-blown First Ministers' Conferences (FMCs), as well as several other meetings. In addition, the provincial premiers met for their Annual Premiers' Conference in August, western premiers met for their annual encounter in May, premiers of the maritime provinces convened on several occasions, and premiers of the eastern provinces met with the governors of the New England states in September 1985.

For every conference involving first ministers, there is at least one, and usually several, meetings of officials. Without exception, these meetings involve and, in most governments, are spearheaded by the people in the intergovernmental affairs agencies. The preparation of briefing books, the coordination of positions among departments, and the attendance at meetings to determine agendas are all duties performed by the specialists in the intergovernmental central agencies. As such, a calendar filled with several meetings of first ministers can greatly enhance the importance of (and the need for) an intergovernmental agency.

Moreover, the convening of an FMC forces governments to coordinate their departments and to arrive at a single government position with respect to the issues on the agenda. A unique FMC was held in 1973, involving the Prime Minister and the Premiers of the four western provinces. This conference, the Western Economic Opportunities Conference (WEOC), was a landmark event, in that it was the first time that provincial premiers were given a forum to discuss federal policies which affected their provinces. It was also an important event for the internal organization of the four participating provincial governments. These governments were required to have – some for the first time – a coordinated position on a variety of issues. To some extent, the WEOC was an impetus to the creation of strong and substantial intergovernmental affairs agencies in some of the western provinces. Howard Leeson writes, with respect to Saskatchewan, that "the WEOC conference of 1973 clearly demonstrated the inadequacy of existing agencies in Saskatchewan designed to support and control intergovernmental relations contact, precipitating the establishment of a central agency with a mandate to coordinate much of this contact."[31]

2. The Organization in Other Governments

The structure of an intergovernmental affairs agency can be affected by policies and structures in another government. For example, the organization of the federal bureaucracy as it relates to regional development policy has had a major impact on the organization within some of the provincial governments. The creation of the federal Department of Regional Economic Expansion (DREE) in 1969 and the establishment of General Development Agreements (GDAs) in the 1970s had important implications for provincial intergovernmental affairs agencies and the organization of provincial bureaucracies generally.

The impact was probably the greatest in the Atlantic provinces. Donald Savoie has noted that the GDA approach was instrumental in centralizing decision-making in certain provincial governments.[32] In dealing with DREE and other federal departments, provinces had little choice but to establish some form of centralized planning or coordinating capability. Otherwise, it would have been left to DREE to provide an overview of GDA activities in the province. Provincial governments would have risked having line departments competing to strike the best deal with DREE.

Anthony Careless has observed that DREE's forceful behaviour in the intergovernmental setting had a profound effect upon the planning and coordinating capacity of the poorer provinces.[33] DREE established what Careless calls "a very definite *style*" for provincial participation; the design, performance and goals of joint programs were to be in accord with federal criteria. As a result, the provinces – dependent on the federal funds – had little room for their own strategic planning and setting of priorities.

The GDAs stipulated that each province had to nominate one minister to act as the provincial counterpart to the minister of DREE and one official to act as the focal point for all agreements. In many of the governments, the individual chosen for this function was from the intergovernmental affairs agency.

A similar requirement was included in the provisions of Economic and Regional Development Agreements (ERDAs), signed between the federal government and all provinces between 1983 and 1985. In several provincial governments, the intergovernmental affairs agency continues to play the coordinating role for ERDA and its subsidiary agreements. At the federal level, the Department of Regional Industrial Expansion assumes responsibility for these agreements.

In 1977, an Urban Affairs and Housing division was created in Alberta's Department of Federal and Intergovernmental Affairs. This division was established directly in response to the federal government's involvement in urban affairs.[34] The Alberta government was concerned that the public would be confused about which level of government was responsible for municipal affairs. This division was later disbanded, after Ottawa's enthusiasm for this area of policy waned.

There was pressure on some governments during the 1970s to establish intergovernmental affairs agencies because other governments had done so. It became apparent to many governments that to be "plugged into" the intergovernmental network, a single central agency or department was required. Central agency intergovernmental specialists in one government interact mostly with their counterparts in other governments. Rarely do they contact officials from the sectoral departments in other governments.

Political Situation
The particular shape that a government's intergovernmental affairs agenda takes at any point in time may reflect elements of the political situation in the country. The importance of such an agency ebbs and flows with various political phenomena. For example, the extent of informal liaison among the staff of the premier's and prime minister's offices and, indeed, among the first ministers themselves, fluctuates. It might be enhanced by a common party label among many of the governments

in power, although the role of partisanship in intergovernmental relations is difficult to determine.

Another political phenomenon which can affect the role of an intergovernmental affairs agency is the length of time a government has been in power. Often, an intergovernmental agency tends to have a significant impact immediately after a change in government. For example, following his accession to power in June 1985, Premier David Peterson in Ontario relied heavily on the Ministry of Intergovernmental Affairs (MIA) to brief him and his neophyte ministers on intergovernmental relations. In a letter sent in August 1985 to all ministers and deputies explaining the role of MIA, sectoral departments were asked to consult MIA on virtually every occasion when they interacted significantly with another government. Conversely, governments that have been in power for several years, such as Bill Davis' in Ontario from 1970 to 1985 and Richard Hatfield's in New Brunswick from 1970 to the present, often gain an adeptness in handling intergovernmental issues and come to rely less heavily on the intergovernmental officials.

Summary
Bureaucratic institutions are not formed in a vacuum. The way governments organize their intergovernmental affairs is in a constant state of flux, continually responding to numerous factors — both external and internal to the government. A plethora of factors has an impact on the structure, size, power, and functions of intergovernmental affairs agencies. As such, what is appropriate for one government may not be appropriate for another. Furthermore, the structures that a government establishes at one time may be inappropriate for another. What needs to be determined is whether the variety and changes that affect the organization of intergovernmental affairs are more important than the common factors that initially led governments to establish intergovernmental central agencies.

In light of the wide variation in structures, functions and powers of intergovernmental relations agencies, to what extent are these bodies similar? On one hand, all governments in Canada have chosen to create an office, department or other agency for the sole purpose of coordinating relations with other governments. This similarity takes on a greater significance, since it appears that the creation of agencies such as these has not developed to nearly the same extent in other federations. Separate departments and offices, as have developed in a number of the Canadian jurisdictions, appear to be a uniquely "Canadian" way of organizing within governments. But the variation in structural organization across the country reflects different regional and provincial cultures, philosophies, population sizes, and fiscal capacities and objectives of the governments.

Donald Wallace suggests that the differences among departments responsible for intergovernmental affairs in the various governments are not as great as they appear.

Despite outward differences in style or approach, similarities can be identified between particular provincial central agencies for intergovernmental relations. Even with significantly less stringent legal mandates and markedly less resources, some central agencies for intergovernmental relations are able to achieve comparable policy effects as their 'stronger' counterparts. [35]

This conclusion is especially interesting in light of arguments and analyses that highlight the differences between intergovernmental affairs agencies, most notably between those that have a statutory basis and those that do not. It has been asserted that central agencies get their power from legislation and/or from control over other agencies and departments. Timothy Woolstencroft writes:

A strong legal foundation provides the agency with the requisite levers to gain access to program information and to require program officials to consult the intergovernmental specialists. A statutory base allows intergovernmental agencies to influence the broad framework and the substantive aspects of government policy. Without such a base, program departments are able to ignore the coordinating agency's efforts to bring some coherence to the government's policies and programs.[36]

With respect to Ontario at the beginning of the 1980s, the ability of the Ministry of Intergovernmental Affairs, "to regulate Ontario's intergovernmental activities is weakened by lack of statute or set of regulations, such as the legislation that created FIGA [in Alberta], which legally requires the participation of the central agency in all intergovernmental negotiations."[37]

However, the goal of central agencies may not be control *per se*. In the discussion on power, it was suggested that one measure of a successful central agency was that it was heeded when it presented an alternate view or proposal. This can be achieved without having complete control over other agencies. Moreover, intergovernmental affairs departments that have strong legislation have tended to rely less on statutory power, and more on their track record and expertise in order to influence the policy-making process.

Despite the variety of forms and bases, it appears that the differences in the influence exerted by intergovernmental agencies in most governments are not that great. Population size is one important factor in determining the nature of the intergovernmental agency. Small units in some of the smaller governments have been able to exercise a comparable degree of control and coordination as have many of the full departments in the larger governments. The smaller units have relied almost exclusively on their location in Executive Council Offices and, thereby, their proximity to the cabinet and first minister for their power.

Notes

1. *Report of the Royal Commission on Government Organization*, vol. 5, Ottawa: Queen's Printer, 1963, pp. 41-2.
2. P. Aucoin and H. Bakvis, "Regional Responsiveness and Government Organization: The Case of Regional

Economic Development Policy in Canada." in P. Aucoin, ed. *Regional Responsiveness and the National Administrative State*. Toronto: University of Toronto Press (Volume 37, Royal Commission on the Economic Union and Development Prospects for Canada research study), 1985, p. 53.

3. Howard Leeson, "Accommodative Mechanisms in a Decentralizing Federation: The Intergovernmental Affairs Function in Saskatchewan." Presented to the Institute for Public Administration, St. John's, 30 August 1985, p. 5.

4. Roger Gibbins, *Conflict and Unity. An Introduction to Canadian Political Life*. Toronto: Methuen, 1985, p. 248.

5. Donald J. Savoie, *Regional Economic Development: Canada's Search for Solutions*. Toronto: University of Toronto Press, 1986, p. 17.

6. Van Loon and Whittington, *The Canadian Political System. Environment, Structure, and Process. Third Edition*. Toronto: McGraw-Hill Ryerson Ltd., 1981, p. 548.

7. Michael Jenkin, *The Challenge of Diversity. Industrial Policy in the Canadian Federation*. Background Study No. 50, Ottawa: Science Council of Canada, 1983, p. 123.

8. D.V. Smiley, *Canada in Question: Federalism in the Eighties. Third Edition,* Toronto: McGraw-Hill Ryerson Ltd., 1980, p. 111.

9. Donald C. Wallace, "Provincial Central Agencies for Intergovernmental Relations and the Policy Process." (unpublished Ph.D dissertation, York University), 1985, p. 19.

10. Richard Simeon, *Federal-Provincial Diplomacy. The Making of Recent Policy in Canada*. Toronto: University of Toronto Press, 1972, p. 37.

11. Gibbins, p. 232.

12. Timothy Woolstencroft, *Organizing Intergovernmental Relations*. Kingston: Institute of Intergovernmental Relations, 1982, p. 76.

13. Wallace, p. 35.

14. Wallace, p. 35.

15. Government of Alberta, Department of Federal and Intergovernmental Affairs, *Tenth Annual Report,* 1984, p. 6.
16. D.V. Smiley, "Public Sector Politics, Modernization and Federalism: The Canadian and American Experiences." *Publius. The Journal of Federalism* 14:1, 1984, p. 58.
17. Smiley, 1980, p. 114.
18. Timothy Woolstencroft, "Intergovernmental Emissaries - The Provincial Guardians of the Federal Bargain: A Case Study of Alberta and Ontario" (unpublished M.A. thesis, Queen's University), 1980, p. 143.
19. Norman Riddell, "Commentary on Future Trends in Canadian Federalism." Presented to the Plenary Session, Annual Conference of the Institute of Public Administration of Canada, St. John's, Newfoundland, August 1985.
20. Volume 3, 1985, p. 264.
21. Carol Goar, *Toronto Star,* 12 October 1985, p. B1.
22. Smiley, 1980, p. 97.
23. C. Campbell and G. Szablowski, *The Superbureaucrats: Structure and Behaviour in Central Agencies.* Toronto: Macmillan of Canada, 1979, p. 8.
24. Woolstencroft, 1982, p. 76.
25. see Leeson, pp. 13-4.
26. Van Loon and Whittington, p. 508.
27. Woolstencroft, 1980, p. 125.
28. Wallace, p. 362.
29. Richard Simeon, "Intergovernmental Relations in Canada Today - Summary of Discussions." in R. Simeon, ed. *Confrontation and Collaboration - Intergovernmental Relations in Canada Today.* Toronto: The Institute of Public Administration of Canada, 1979, p. 3.
30. Government of Canada. "Progress Report on Federal-Provincial Relations." Prepared for the Annual Conference of First Ministers, Halifax, November 28-29, 1985, p. 16.
31. Leeson, p. 9.
32. Savoie, Donald J. "The GDA Approach and the Bureaucratization of Provincial Governments in the

Atlantic Provinces." *Canadian Public Administration*, 24:1, 1981, p. 128.
33. Anthony Careless, *Initiative and Response. The Adaption of Canadian Federalism to Regional Economic Development*. Montreal: The Institute of Public Administration of Canada, 1977, p. 168.
34. Woolstencroft, 1980, p. 109
35. Wallace, p. 378.
36. Woolstencroft, 1982, pp. 16-7.
37. Woolstencroft, 1980, p. 134.

4 IMPACT

It has been observed that many factors affect the development of an intergovernmental affairs agency. Characteristics within the government itself and in society generally can have an impact on the structure, power and nature of an agency.

However, there is a two-way relationship between an agency and the world in which it is situated. The impact of an intergovernmental affairs agency can be felt in various ways. The following discussion will be divided into those effects felt within the government of which the agency is a part and those effects which ripple through its liaison with other governments.

The Impact on the Intragovernmental World

The rise of intergovernmental affairs agencies has had an impact on the relations and operations within a government in several ways. These include: an increase in the size of governments, the creation of a new type of government official, and a readjustment of relations among government departments and agencies.

Size of Governments
Perhaps most basic, the size of many governments has been increased simply because an additional agency has

been created. In several governments, the intergovernmental affairs unit is a full department, comparable in size to some smaller sectoral departments, although it is possible that in the absence of a separate central agency for intergovernmental relations, governments would have increased the number of people specializing in intergovernmental relations within existing line departments.

Type of Official

A second effect has been the creation of a new type of official. The work of the intergovernmental affairs official is unique:

> The process experts who work in these agencies are perhaps a new breed of public servant. They do not deal directly with substantive matters but rather develop strategies, coordinate policy and program activities across their respective governments and maintain liaison with their counterparts in other governments. [1]

Another unique quality of intergovernmental affairs specialists who work in central agencies is a high level of "politicization". Kenneth Kernaghan defines "politicization" as the process by which officials become increasingly involved in politics either in the partisan sense or in the broader sense of the authoritative allocation of values for society. [2]

Audrey Doerr writes that the fact that the activities of intergovernmental specialists are "so closely tied to political negotiations and are conducted from departments and offices that play a central coordinative role within the particular government emphasizes the importance of process expertise." [3] Many intergovernmental officials are devoted to general issues of policy and strategy, primarily as backup for the more political meetings of ministers and premiers. [4]

Intragovernmental Relations

The creation of a central agency for *inter*governmental relations has implications for a government's *intra*governmental relations — the relations among the agencies and departments within a government. A central agency inevitably comes into some conflict with sectorally-defined departments. Virtually by definition, central agencies tread on the turf of sectoral departments. The extent of that conflict varies from government to government and from department to department.

Conflict within governments involving inter-governmental affairs agencies can be of two sorts. First, friction can develop with line departments or other central agencies engaged in intergovernmental duties. Second, there can be competition with other departments and agencies over which objectives the government should be pursuing.

1. Conflict Over Intergovernmental Functions

In governments in Canada, both central agencies and line departments are engaged in intergovernmental relations. Intergovernmental affairs are now practiced by specialists in several of the line departments in all governments. The extent to which formal federal-provincial units exist in sectoral departments varies greatly from government to government. In part, it depends on the existence and size of a separate intergovernmental affairs central agency.

Some governments have formal intergovernmental units in several departments, whereas others have them in only one or two. The size and importance of these units varies greatly as well. In some governments, these line department units have larger budgets than the intergovernmental affairs department or agency.

The interface between governments is dominated by thousands of contacts between technicians. Functional contacts are maintained on a continual basis between sectoral department officials. Hundreds of very specific agreements are administered by these officials. These relations are more or less indifferent to the political mood of intergovernmental relations. For some line departments, these functional relations are the extent of their intergovernmental relations.

The nature and extent of a sectoral department's role in federal-provincial matters is at times difficult to determine. Some departments have formal units for intergovernmental relations — which may be involved in strategic planning and intergovernmental policy formulation — whereas others have branches that perform similar functions, but this is not reflected in the name. Intergovernmental specialists in the line departments can be difficult to track down. Often there is no indication in their title that they are involved primarily in intergovernmental relations. Kenneth Kernaghan has noted that there are essentially two types of people in line departments who make an important contribution to intergovernmental affairs.[5] There are senior officials in operating departments who have responsibility for intergovernmental issues affecting their department. Second, there are senior officials who devote relatively little time to intergovernmental issues, but whose occasional involvement has a major influence on the outcome of intergovernmental negotiations.

Unlike the officials who work in intergovernmental agencies, who tend to be "process" specialists but "policy" generalists, the intergovernmental specialists in line departments tend to have substantial expertise in the intergovernmental aspects of one policy field. The extent to which a line department in a government has intergovernmental expertise depends primarily on the subject matter and on the amount of interaction with other governments that is required. It also varies from one government to another. In departments for sectors such as agriculture, energy, and health, requiring a substantial amount of interaction between levels of government, there is more likely to be individuals who specialize in intergovernmental relations.

There can be friction between the intergovernmental affairs agency and some of the sectoral departments. For some departments, the intergovernmental agency can be a nuisance - possibly harming relations built up with officials in the line department of another government. Moreover, the central agency can be a constraining influence, forcing a line department to change its intergovernmental policy in order to be consistent with government-wide objectives.

Most departments would acknowledge that intergovernmental central agencies are useful in providing information on other governments and other sectors, and in preparing strategy and briefing books for First Ministers' Conferences. However, for most line department officials, such activities and information are not of great concern. For the most part, they operate in narrow, functional areas. Relations with other governments, to the extent they are needed, are established within these functional areas. Generally, for them, the intergovernmental affairs agency is a constraint and its impact - to the extent that it exists - detrimental.

Friction within governments involving intergovernmental agencies has most often been with finance or treasury departments. The first steps towards the institutionalization of intergovernmental relations were taken by creating separate federal-provincial divisions within departments of finance. This process began in 1954 with the creation of such a unit in the federal Department of Finance. Virtually by definition, all finance and treasury departments have a unit, either formal or informal, which is engaged in intergovernmental relations.

Finance departments have a special role in intergovernmental affairs. In the 1950s, intergovernmental affairs were dominated by fiscal relations and, as such, the departments of finance in all governments enjoyed almost exclusive power in this area. In Ontario, the intergovernmental affairs ministry was at one point part of the Treasury. Manitoba's approach was for a long time modelled on the example of Ontario's Department of Treasury Economics and Intergovernmental Affairs. Until 1984, the Manitoba government's centre for intergovernmental relations was a branch in the Department of Finance.

The mandate of all provincial finance and treasury departments includes responsibility for funds coming from the federal government. A key objective of those sections of finance and treasury departments concerned with fiscal and intergovernmental relations is the optimization of federal transfer arrangements. Because the transfer of revenue underlies much of intergovernmental interaction, departments of finance inevitably play a central role in this area of activity.

There are certain intergovernmental issues that are predominantly financial. These include the various elements of the Fiscal Arrangements legislation, such as equalization, Established Program Financing (EPF), and tax collection agreements. Even though other policy sectors are often involved, such as health and education in the EPF negotiations, finance departments play the lead role with respect to these issues.

The creation of a separate unit for intergovernmental relations has usually resulted in some limitations on the role of the finance or treasury department. Prior to the creation of intergovernmental units, the finance departments were often involved in virtually all intergovernmental interaction, including some that was clearly beyond their purview. Most finance departments do not object to intergovernmental agencies assuming responsibility for the intergovernmental aspect of non-finance issues. Any friction which results between finance departments and intergovernmental agencies is usually over those issues which are perceived to be primarily of a "finance" nature.

The Report of the Task Force on Government Organization and Employment recognized that in Manitoba, "[the Department of] Finance has an important advisory, monitoring and control responsibility with respect to the financial aspects of line departments' federal-provincial activity."[6] The Report cautioned, however, that although Finance can influence the policy-making role for line departments, "this role should not be primary or absolute." The Report concluded that the Department of Finance "would be an inappropriate place in which to lodge responsibility for reviewing and developing a comprehensive overview of the field [of federal-provincial relations] which would include financial *and* non-financial issues."[7]

After an intergovernmental affairs agency has been in existence for a few years, and has attained a level of stability in the government bureaucracy, friction with other departments and agencies over areas of responsibility usually decreases. Lines of jurisdiction are demarcated and, in most cases, peaceful co-existence develops.

2. Competition Over Government Objectives

A united front by a government in its intergovernmental dealings may conceal conflicts over objectives and strategies within the government. All governments have more than one objective which, when applied to a single issue, may conflict. The Report of the Royal Commission on the Economic Union and Development Prospects for Canada notes that "within the federal government, economic policy makers have different viewpoints, represented by different departments and agencies, each oriented to its own set of policy objectives."[8]

This competition is a normal part of decision-making within all governments. The presence of a separate intergovernmental affairs agency tends to enhance this intragovernmental friction. Such friction relates directly to power and competition for control and input into the decision-making process. Who in a government has the say over intergovernmental policy? Who directs the government's policy in its relations with other governments? Of special concern is how much power (that is, influence) do intergovernmental affairs agencies have?

Conventional wisdom has often dictated that a central agency either has total control or it fails. In explaining why the position of Minister of State for Federal-Provincial Relations was abolished at the federal level in 1980, former Minister John Reid argued that there was no central control: each department pursued its own federal-provincial relations.[9] Donald Wallace argues convincingly against putting so much weight on "bureaucratic centralization" as the only measure of an intergovernmental affairs agency's influence.[10]

The allocation of resources for intergovernmental affairs between central agencies and line departments is one indicator of the distribution of power. It is not conclusive, however. The distribution of funds is at times difficult to ascertain; in some departments it is not clear which units are actively engaged in intergovernmental relations. Even though other departments clearly do have officials working in this area, budget classifications and organizational structures do not enable the resources allocated for the purpose of intergovernmental relations to be determined.

In central agencies, power is measured in terms of being able to make an impact on policy-making. For this to occur, an agency needs access to the policy process: it has to have input into the system. Intergovernmental affairs agencies, however, compete with other agencies and departments, which may have different perspectives and objectives.

Often, the intergovernmental unit acts within its own government as the representative of the other level of government. In a sense, the other governments are the "clientele" of the intergovernmental units. As a result, in policy discussions in cabinet or cabinet committees, the intergovernmental affairs representative often requests that certain policy proposals by other departments be amended because of the effect they would have on other governments.

How much power do these "process" experts actually exert in their intragovernmental relations? Although they do perform a unique role, the influence of officials in central agencies over line departments often tends to be exaggerated. Central agency generalists are often unable to understand, let alone participate, in the complex technical negotiations which characterize much of intergovernmental bargaining.[11] The complexity of most issues requires some reliance upon technical specialists who are usually found in the line departments.

While the expertise of the specialists in intergovernmental affairs agencies may touch upon a wide variety of policy sectors, that knowledge is neither as great nor as intensive as that held by the specialists in the relevant line departments. Furthermore, intergovernmental central agencies, because of their small size and stretched capacities, are often dependent on the sectoral departments for specialized knowledge and advice on policy alternatives.

Expertise is not the only source of a line department's power. Most departments have programs to administer and, as such, have large budgets. In addition, most have clientele groups that provide the political support a government needs to remain in power.

With respect to the federal government, Michael Jenkin concludes that although the Federal-Provincial Relations Office has a coordinating role, ensuring that departments take federal-provincial relations into account in the formulation of policy papers for cabinet, the departments are really free to act on their own on a day-to-day basis.[12] Experience in most governments demonstrates that intergovernmental policy is, for the most part, determined in the line departments.

Timothy Woolstencroft provides an example of how a federal initiative spawned opposing responses among intergovernmental specialists and Treasury officials in Ontario in 1975.[13] The former viewed the federal imposition of wages and price controls and the establishment of the Anti-Inflation Board as intrusions into provincial affairs and, thus, recommended that they be opposed. The fiscal and economic experts in the Treasury department, however, thought the federal measures were necessary and appropriate. The Ontario government supported the federal initiative.

It is clear from other examples, however, that intergovernmental affairs agencies have at times had an impact on the objectives pursued by governments in their interactions with other governments. Perhaps one of the most important effects of the rise of intergovernmental affairs specialists has been the tendency for governments to link issues. Prior to the creation of intergovernmental central agencies, issues were fought, negotiated and dealt with by specialists in the relevant sectors. Issues in other sectors were rarely considered. As a result, two governments could be at loggerheads in one sector, but working harmoniously together in another.

The introduction of linkages into negotiations meant that more than one sector could be under consideration at the same time. Moreover, it meant that a government might trade off success in one issue for partial success in another. The need arose to priorize objectives in all sectors. This has led to some conflict between sectoral departments, whose objectives are traded off or given a lower priority, and the intergovernmental agencies who attempt to determine the best deal for the government as a whole.

Adie and Thomas conclude that what a government hopes to get from intergovernmental negotiations may vary, depending on whether or not there are intergovernmental specialists.[14] It was noted earlier that some observers have suggested that intergovernmental officials tend to define their role exclusively in terms of enhancing the reputation of their governments. As such, they may approach all federal-provincial negotiations with the objective of "winning" rather than trying to identify a compromise solution.

The opposite may also be true. Richard Schultz, for example, has observed that actors from intergovernmental central agencies often hold perspectives that emphasize a desire to establish or maintain a harmonious relationship with other governments.[15] This may be the message that a government carries into its intergovernmental negotiations, even if it conflicts with a particular department's concern with the implementation of a specific program.

This difference in perspectives was observed by Brown and Eastman in their analysis of the 1978 First Ministers' Conferences.[16] The authors noted that intergovernmental affairs specialists were professionally dedicated to the maintenance of the process of intergovernmental discussion. For them, the substance was less important; they knew the issues would return again and again. "Success" was measured not in terms of resolution, but in keeping the lines of communication open.

The presence of central agencies for intergovernmental relations may compel line departments at both levels of government to reach agreements and to resolve problems between them. Richard Simeon has observed that: "Federal and provincial officials often made common cause to promote and protect their programmes against the interference of federal and provincial central agencies.... [They] knew that if they failed to resolve conflicts among themselves, then it would be done by outsiders [that is, intergovernmental affairs agencies] who did not share their programme concerns."[17]

Campbell and Szablowski observe that at the federal level, the Department of Finance presents a particular point of view – that is, the maintenance of the country's economic stability – which does not always mesh with the requirements of political stability, nor with the tactics that the Federal-Provincial Relations Office may want to employ to gain a political advantage over one or more of the provinces, (or to maintain good communications with the provinces).[18]

The Impact on the Intergovernmental World

Richard Simeon has noted that "the institutional arrangements of the constituent governments are a fundamental factor shaping intergovernmental relations in Canada."[19] Stefan Dupré writes that "the intergovernmental relations between elected and appointed officials of our two levels of government are bound to be affected by the very different intragovernmental relations that characterize the departmentalized and institutionalized modes of cabinet operation."[20] In the former type of cabinet, which dominated governments in Canada through the 1950s and early 1960s (the period of "cooperative federalism"), the line ministers had a substantial degree of autonomy and the departments were relatively independent. In the latter – the institutionalized cabinet – there are central agencies and formal committee structures. Shared knowledge, collegial decision-making and the formulation of government-wide priorities and objectives are emphasized. Intergovernmental agencies are one component of this type of cabinet organization that appeared in Canadian governments in the late 1960s and 1970s.

Volume of Interaction

As noted in the previous section on intragovernmental relations, a government's objectives and negotiating tactics have implications for intergovernmental negotiations. Furthermore, it has been argued that the increase in the amount of intergovernmental machinery generally, including intergovernmental affairs agencies, has led to the proliferation of intergovernmental conferences and meetings.[21] It is difficult, though, to determine how much of the substantial increase in the volume of intergovernmental interaction can be attributed to the presence of intergovernmental affairs agencies. The change in the public agenda and the rise of numerous issues involving jurisdictional and constitutional questions made increased interaction inevitable. In fact, in Chapter Three, it was suggested that the increased interaction was actually a cause behind the creation of intergovernmental affairs agencies.

Conflict or Accommodation
Finally, it has been argued that the presence of intergovernmental affairs agencies has an effect on the "mood" of intergovernmental relations — the level of conflict and the likelihood of accommodation in the federal-provincial arena. A discussion of conflict in the system must begin with the observation that there are two distinct types of conflict. Some conflict and differences in objectives and positions among the various governments in Canada, is inevitable, if not desirable. Intergovernmental tensions are inherent in Canadian federalism. Ideally, these should be managed "prudently and productively".[22] At times, however, a second type of conflict has pervaded the federal system. It is characterized by acrimonious relations and little effort to manage productively the tensions between governments. Such conflict has often been gratuitous. The present discussion is focused on conflict that approaches the latter definition.

A point can also be inserted about intergovernmental relations and conflict at the functional as opposed to the political level. It has already been noted that intergovernmental relations in Canada involves literally hundreds of contacts between officials in different governments. The vast majority of these contacts is made by lower level officials in the line departments with their counterparts in the other governments. Most of

92

these are very narrow and technical. Much of the interaction relates to the administration of several hundred intergovernmental agreements which have been negotiated between two or more governments in Canada.

In large measure, the functional relations between governments are impervious to the shifts in conflict-cooperation that tend to affect federal-provincial relations at a political level. Regardless of a government's stance towards the other level of government, these functional contacts continue to be made. A striking example concerns Quebec, which officially boycotted federal-provincial meetings in the years following the partial constitutional accord of November 1981. During these years, functional relations between officials in Quebec and Ottawa continued to go on much as before.

There are essentially two competing arguments with respect to the relationship between structure and conflict in the system. The premise of both is that intergovernmental organization can affect the level of conflict and the likelihood of accommodation. Following is a summary of each of the two arguments.

Proposition 1:   Intergovernmental Affairs Agencies
                  Enhance Conflict

According to this perspective, the existence — and growth — of intergovernmental affairs specialty units during the 1970s actually exacerbated the level of conflict in federal-provincial relations. The more political the structure, the less likely it is that accommodation can be reached. It is generally recognized that if an issue becomes politicized, quiet negotiations among officials become very difficult. It can be argued that the structures themselves contribute to this politicization of intergovernmental issues simply by being close to the first minister or the cabinet. It may be that central agencies are inherently more political than line departments. Stefan Dupré suggests that while central agencies *per se* are not inimical to the conduct of functional (and therefore, cooperative) relations, their role should be limited to communicating or clarifying general policy.[23] Once central agencies are fully involved in an issue, it usually ensures that it will become a "summit" (and therefore, a political) issue.

It has been argued that the rationalization of government processes, which preoccupied many governments during the 1960s and 1970s, was one cause of increased federal-provincial conflict in the ensuing years. Chapter Three noted that, in several governments, the rise of intergovernmental affairs units and other central agencies was an integral part of this rationalization process. The adoption of such a process often led to the creation of comprehensive plans. When two governments approached one another in areas of joint activity with broad, preconceived plans, conflict was heightened.

Michael Jenkin suggests that successful inter-governmental negotiations depend in part on the degree to which governments are flexible about achieving objectives, and the degree to which they are willing to involve the other level at an early stage.[24] The rationalization process seems diametrically opposed to this recipe for successful negotiations. Related to this, it can be asserted that the mere existence of intergovernmental affairs agencies can enhance an atmosphere of conflict because they provide a locus where past injustices and jurisdictional issues can be nurtured.

A second aspect of this relationship between intergovernmental affairs agencies and enhanced conflict concerns the forces that motivate officials who work in these agencies. It has been argued that the presence of intergovernmental affairs specialists can increase the likelihood of conflict. Three broad reasons have been offered.

First, as has been argued by Donald Smiley, intergovernmental specialists in each government are concerned primarily with the protection of their government's jurisdiction, rather than with the resolution of problems, thereby making negotiations more difficult and conflict more likely. "In his stance toward other governments the federal-provincial relations specialist has a single-minded devotion to the power of his jurisdiction. And because his counterparts in other governments have the same motivations, conflict is inevitable."[25]

A second and related explanation is that conflict in the intergovernmental arena enhances the role of the intergovernmental specialists. It is easier to justify the presence of process specialists when problems are perceived than when relations are running smoothly.

Third, it has been argued that the trust ties and shared norms, which were an important part of "cooperative federalism" in the late 1950s and 1960s, are absent when federal-provincial relations are dominated by officials of central agencies. There are various elements in the shared-cost relationship that served to promote accommodation.

Program specialists tended to share common frames of reference — similar attitudes, procedures and values. Federal-provincial cooperation was facilitated by long-standing friendships. Officials from the federal and provincial governments benefitted from the shared-cost programs. They shared common outlooks, met frequently, created programs that expanded their authority, developed client and special interest group support, and often appeared to circumvent control by the elected policy makers.[26] These elements are less important in the period dominated by "executive federalism".

As a corollary, Audrey Doerr has argued that the increase in the number of actors and structures, and the corresponding elaboration of intergovernmental processes, has created a complicated web of interrelationships within and between governments.[27] This in itself has raised the level of conflict in the system.

Proposition 2:   Intergovernmental Affairs Agencies
                   Diminish Conflict

That the rise of intergovernmental agencies and specialists is a cause of conflict is not universally accepted. Contrary to the position just presented, a second position states that the presence of intergovernmental specialists has actually increased the likelihood of accommodation.

It can be argued that the rationalization which has taken place in many governments — of which the rise of intergovernmental affairs agencies is an integral part — has been more directed toward consensus than conflict. It removes sporadic elements from the decision-making process and introduces elements of predictability.

With respect to the intergovernmental specialists, Kenneth Kernaghan notes that the extent to which these officials have been concerned with guarding their government's jurisdiction varies greatly from government to government, and from official to official.[28] There is nothing inherent in the position which leads to taking a stance that will enhance the level of conflict.

The objectives of these central agency specialists are often geared towards accommodation. Keeping the lines of communication open is often a goal in itself. This requires some give and take with counterparts in other governments. Donald Smiley implies that the shared values and norms which dominated relations between program officials during the 1950s and 1960s are absent from the current era of intergovernmental relations.[29] However, a network of personal contacts has developed among officials of intergovernmental agencies. This personal comaraderie is very helpful for successful negotiations.

A case study by Donald Wallace illustrates that with respect to international activity, provincial government central agencies for intergovernmental relations have gone a considerable distance towards facilitating harmonious and collaborative federal-provincial liaison.[30] Intergovernmental specialists have, at times, acted as a referee for intergovernmental conflict between line departments of two governments.

Conclusion
Based on the above discussion, a good case can be made that the presence of intergovernmental affairs agencies do not necessarily lead to enhanced conflict in the system. There is no inherent link between this type of agency and conflict in the federal-provincial arena. This does not rule out the possibility that some officials in some agencies, in their pursuit of defending their

government's jurisdiction, have heightened the level of conflict among governments.

However, this debate may be too narrowly focused. Two points can be made. First, the impact that these agencies can have on the extent of conflict and acrimony among governments is necessarily small. Regardless of the impact of intergovernmental affairs agencies on the mood of relations, it must be acknowledged that conflict between governments is due primarily to other factors. Second, intergovernmental harmony itself is not a major objective of governments and, as such, agencies should not be evaluated according to whether or not they contribute to conflict.

With respect to the first, many of the issues on the recent intergovernmental agenda are essentially conflictual. Richard Simeon writes: "Conflict stems not just from administrative weaknesses but from real differences in goals and priorities."[31] The issues which have risen to the top of the public agenda in recent years have tended to be territorially based, pitting regions of the country against one another. Alan Cairns suggests that territorially-based conflicts, because they directly engage the power, status and goals of rival governments, are more difficult to resolve than functionally-based ones.[32] Conflict of this sort in Canada has often manifested itself as federal-provincial conflict.

It can be argued that the current mechanisms of liaison, such as First Ministers' Conferences, are inadequate to resolve such conflict. They are often public, thereby encouraging the practice of "grandstanding" by first ministers. Morever, it can be argued that there is no incentive to reach accommodation and no mechanism to resolve an impasse.

Second, it is not enough to evaluate intergovernmental agencies simply in terms of their impact on the level of conflict in the federal-provincial arena. If these agencies have served to increase the level of conflict in federal-provincial relations, then their effect has been, at least in part, deleterious. However, even if this could be illustrated, there may be another effect which more than offsets this negative impact. It might be argued that the increased conflict which has resulted is simply a side effect which ought to be endured because of some benefit which accrues from the presence of intergovernmental agencies. As a result, it is wrong to focus exclusively on whether or not there has been an increased level of conflict. Intergovernmental harmony is not an objective in itself, except to the extent that it can enhance the fulfillment of policy objectives.

Notes

1. Audrey Doerr, "Public Administration: Federalism and Intergovernmental Relations." in K. Kernaghan, ed. *Canadian Public Administration: Discipline and Profession*. Toronto: Butterworths, 1983, p. 132.
2. Kernaghan, Kenneth. "The Power and Responsibility of Intergovernmental Officials in Canada." prepared for the Annual Conference of the Institute of Public Administration of Canada, Winnipeg, August 1979, p. 17.
3. Doerr, p. 178.
4. Simeon, Richard. *The Federal-Provincial Decision Making Process*. Intergovernmental Relations. Issues and Alternatives 1977. Toronto: Ontario Economic Council, 1977, p. 31.
5. Kernaghan, pp. 2-3.
6. Government of Manitoba. *Report of the Task Force on Government Organization and Economy*, 31 March 1978, p. 94.
7. Government of Manitoba, p. 97.
8. Volume 3, 1985, p. 148.
9. From Canadian Study of Parliament Group, Seminar on First Ministers' Conferences, Halifax, May 1981, p. 14.
10. Donald C. Wallace, *Provincial Central Agencies for Intergovernmental Relations and the Policy Process*, (unpublished Ph.D. dissertation, York University), 1985, p. 350.
11. See R. Schultz, "Prime Ministerial Government, Central Agencies, and Operating Departments: Towards a More Realistic Analysis." in T.A. Hockin,

ed. *Apex of Power. The Prime Minister and Political Leadership in Canada, 2nd. Edition*. Scarborough: Prentice-Hall of Canada Ltd., 1977, p. 234.

12. Micheal Jenkin, *The Challenge of Diversity. Industrial Policy in the Canadian Federation*. Background Study No. 50. Ottawa: Science Council of Canada, 1983, p. 164.

13. Timothy Woolstencroft, *Intergovernmental Emissaries - The Provincial Guardians of the Federal Bargain: A Case Study of Alberta and Ontario*, (unpublished M.A. theses, Queen's University), 1980, P. 129.

14. Adie and Thomas, *Canadian Public Administration. Problematic Perspectives*, Scarborough: Prentice-Hall, 1982, p. 247.

15. Schultz, p. 234.

16. Brown and Eastman, *The Limits of Consultation. A Debate Among Ottawa, the Provinces and the Private Sector on an Industrial Strategy*. Ottawa: Science Council of Canada, 1981, p. 63.

17. Simeon, Richard. *Federal-Provincial Diplomacy: The Making of Recent Policy in Canada*, Toronto: University of Toronto Press, 1972, pp. 36-37.

18. Campbell and Szablowski, *The Superbureaucrats: Structure and Behaviour in Central Agencies.*, Toronto: The Institute of Public Administration of Canada, 1979, p. 51 (The part in brackets is added.)

19. Simeon, 1972, p. 38.

20. Dupré, J. Stefan. "Reflections on the Workability of Executive Federalism." in R. Simeon, ed. *Intergovernmental Relations*, Toronto: University of Toronto Press, (Vol. 63, Royal Commission on the Economic Union and Development Prospects for Canada research study), 1985, p. 5.

21. Kenneth Kernaghan, "Intergovernmental Administrative Relations in Canada." in K. Kernaghan, ed. *Public Administration in Canada, Selected Readings, 4th ed*, Toronto: Methuen, 1982, p. 81.

22. Government of Canada. "Progress Report on Federal-Provincial Relations." Prepared for the Annual Conference of First Ministers, Halifax, November 28-29, 1985, p. 2.

23. Dupré, p. 23.

24. Jenkin, p. 104.
25. D.V. Smiley, "An Outsider's Observations of Federal-Provincial Relations Among Consenting Adults." in R. Simeon, ed. *Conflict and Collaboration - Intergovernmental Relations in Canada Today*. Toronto: The Institute of Public Administration of Canada, 1979, p. 109.
26. D.V. Smiley, "Public Administration and Canadian Federalism." in J.P. Meekison, ed. *Canadian Federalism: Myth or Reality?* Toronto: Methuen, 1968, pp. 278-9.
27. Doerr, p. 180.
28. Kernaghan, 1982, p. 89.
29. D.V. Smiley, "Federal-Provincial Conflict in Canada." *Publius. The Journal of Federalism*. Vol. 4, 1974, p. 21.
30. Wallace, p. 379
31. Simeon, 1977, p. 37.
32. Alan C. Cairns. "The Governments and Societies of Canadian Federalism." *Canadian Journal of Political Science*, Vol. X:4, December 1977, p. 720.

5 EVALUATION

This study has focused on the intergovernmental affairs agencies that have existed, at least for a period, in all federal, provincial, and territorial governments. Chapter One described the evolution of these intergovernmental affairs agencies and Chapter Two addressed the various functions which they perform and the powers they exercise. Chapter Three attempted to explain the great variety among them while Chapter Four explored the impact that they have had — both on the intragovernmental scene and with respect to the world of intergovernmental affairs.

Intergovernmental interaction is not an end in itself. Rather, it is a means of achieving certain policy objectives. It is these objectives that provide the most important criteria by which to evaluate intergovernmental agencies. Although, in theory, intergovernmental relations are not essential for a government to formulate policy, it would be nearly impossible for a government in Canada to achieve its policy objectives without interacting with other governments. The nature of the Canadian constitution and the resulting interdependence of governments has meant that in many sectors, a government either does not have the constitutional authority or the financial resources to do all that it wishes in order to achieve certain objectives.

Furthermore, in other sectors, often the impact of a particular policy will so extensively affect another government that proceeding unilaterally could seriously damage relations with that government.

Some of the most important policy objectives of governments in Canada have necessitated interacting with other governments. To assist in attaining these objectives, all governments have created intergovernmental affairs agencies. What contribution have these agencies made to the achievement of intergovernmental policy? How essential have these agencies been? Have they helped or hindered governments in the attainment of their policy objectives?

In Chapter Two, a long list of functions performed by at least some intergovernmental affairs agencies was enumerated. Some of these functions could be – and, in some governments are – performed by other agencies and departments in the government. For example, responsibility for international relations may be divided between the line department for trade relations and the first minister's office. Many of the policy areas for which intergovernmental agencies have assumed responsibility from time to time may be integrated into line departments. Cabinet secretariat functions are, in most governments, handled by the office of the first minister.

There is a group of unique functions, however, that would not be performed if an intergovernmental affairs unit did not exist. Essentially, these functions define such a unit. Most important are those activities related to the coordination of intergovernmental affairs. These functions should be considered when evaluating the importance of intergovernmental agencies.

Intergovernmental Objectives

A government may hold several possible objectives related to coordination in the area of intergovernmental affairs. The following section will, first, outline these goals and, second, assess the role of the intergovernmental affairs agencies in assisting their governments in meeting them.

Three broad intergovernmental objectives can be identified. First is the goal of a broad, comprehensive intergovernmental strategy. Second is the attempt either to obtain funding from another government or to establish a policy in an area that requires the cooperation of another government. The third objective of a government relates to the protection of its jurisdiction.

Intergovernmental Policy Formulation
Perhaps foremost, a government may wish to have a comprehensive, "directed" policy on intergovernmental relations in order to "manage the interface". This is a broad objective that may have several components. Implicit is the notion of strategic, long-term planning. The Report of the Task Force on Government Organization and Economy in Manitoba observed that the established practice there of making line departments responsible for the development and administration of federal-provincial programs,

> may insulate programmes from scrutiny and, perhaps more seriously, militate against the development of our overall, comprehensive view on the part of any person or group in government. [1]

The Report asks: "Without such an overview, how are the relative priorities of the government to be determined; how can governmental, as opposed to a departmental point of view on the overall objectives of the system be achieved?"[2]
It is important that this function be performed by an agency that is not tied to a narrow "line department" perspective. Intergovernmental affairs agencies are ideally placed to develop government-wide policies on intergovernmental relations. They are not attached to a particular viewpoint or clientele. Furthermore, they monitor intergovernmental relations across the spectrum of policy sectors, enabling them to ensure that objectives in the intergovernmental arena are consistent with the overall policy goals of the government. This capacity reduces the likelihood of sectoral departments reaching agreements with another government, or behaving in some fashion which is inconsistent with the government's priorities and goals.

The success of intergovernmental affairs agencies in policy formulation and planning has varied among governments. It has depended largely on the resources granted to an agency for this purpose. These, in turn, reflect a government's support both for strategic planning generally and for the intergovernmental agency's role in such a task. Clearly, without the support of the first minister, and without the allocation of sufficient resources, agencies are unable to be engaged in comprehensive intergovernmental policy formulation in any significant way.

Timothy Woolstencroft has suggested that central coordination is of concern primarily to those governments that are dissatisfied with their stake in the federation.[3] The implication is that in a period of acrimony, it is more important that there be a unit to perform this "top-down" coordinating role. Howard Leeson suggests that one reason for the Saskatchewan government disbanding the Department of Intergovernmental Affairs in 1983 was that it had decided on "a more cooperative, less conflictual style of relationship with the federal government."[4]

An alternate view also exists. Coordination may be equally important in a period of cooperation, but for a different reason. According to this perspective, when federal-provincial harmony is seen as essential to achieving intergovernmental policy objectives, then it is important that all communications and interaction with the other governments be effective. At the root of this perspective is an acceptance of the fact that governments in Canada have, and will continue to have different objectives and approaches. Even in a period of cooperation, these often collide. When governments expect to achieve concrete results from their intergovernmental liaison – as they do in a period of cooperation – there is an increased volume of interaction. The need to manage the difference among governments becomes paramount.

An examination of intergovernmental affairs agencies in the Saskatchewan government and in other governments that disbanded departments in recent years suggests that concern with coordination has not diminished as a result of the structural changes. In fact, central coordination may be an even greater priority in the current "era of cooperation", and more easily managed from these agencies located close to the premier.

Obtaining Funds and Cooperation

A second major objective that governments have in the area of intergovernmental liaison relates to obtaining either funds or cooperation from another government. With respect to the former, provincial and territorial governments are dependent, in varying degrees, on federal transfer payments. The primary sources of these are from equalization payments (for some provinces) and from the Established Programs Financing payments – for health and hospital insurance and post-secondary education programs. Both of these transfers to provinces (totalling over 14 billion dollars in 1985-86[5]) are the result of fiscal arrangements negotiated every five years in multilateral federal-provincial sessions. One objective of the provinces is to ensure that these payments are not curbed and that revenues remain predictable.

Another source of federal funds is provided through regional development agreements. Under umbrella Economic and Regional Development Agreements, all provinces have negotiated conditional subsidiary agreements with the federal government which provide for both governments to contribute funds for development in a particular sector or region.

In addition to aquiring revenue, governments often need to obtain the cooperation of other governments in order to meet certain of their own specific policy goals. This cooperation may take a variety of forms. It may involve the federal spending power, such that provincial governments require federal assistance to be able to finance programs in sectors within their jurisdiction. Conversely, the federal government may have objectives that require provincial cooperation, such as the attainment of national standards of services within provincial jurisdictions. Provincial governments may have goals that necessarily require federal cooperation because of some extra-provincial effect of their policy.

Cooperation may involve the agreement between two orders of government concerning the administration of a joint program. Or it may involve the delegation of responsibility from one government to another. For example, the Atlantic Accord, signed between the Governments of Canada and Newfoundland, delegated some responsibility for managing the offshore resources to the provincial government, even though these are within federal jurisdiction.

Intergovernmental agreements are the principal vehicle for obtaining revenues from another government, or for getting a policy implemented in an area within the jurisdiction of another government. All governments hope to maximize their benefits in agreements with other governments, and since agreements with other governments are reached through negotiations, the better a government is at negotiating, the more beneficial the agreement that it can reach.

Intergovernmental affairs agencies are able to assist their governments in developing strategy in negotiating and in reaching agreements. Moreover, because of their role as monitors, they can link developments and issues in one sector to developments in another. They are also aware of other agreements, perhaps with other governments and perhaps in other sectors, which may set a precedent for what their government is attempting to achieve. They are experts on intergovernmental agreements, aware of their various nuances, forms, and legal and constitutional implications. They are also experts in negotiating and in maintaining connections with the "negotiators" in other governments. This combination of knowledge, skills and contact enables them to develop innovative alternate arrangements in the event of a stalemate. For the most part, line agencies have found that intergovernmental affairs officials have helped them in maximizing their objectives (financial and jurisdictional) in negotiations.

Officials in intergovernmental affairs agencies can help to ensure that agreements are consistent with the overall objectives of the government. Stefan Dupré, in prescribing a "workable executive federalism", argues that while the role of central agencies in federal-provincial interaction should be limited, such agencies should make "occasional appearances" for the purpose of communicating or clarifying general policy. Dupré argues that ongoing participation in the process of consultation or negotiations should be the preserve of sectoral department officials.

Protection of Jurisdiction

The third broad objective arising from a government's interaction with other governments relates to the protection of jurisdiction. In establishing intergovernmental affairs departments or agencies, some provincial governments explicitly stated that they were combatting incursions by the federal government into areas of provincial jurisdiction. This goal is perhaps the most controversial objective of governments in the intergovernmental realm. The extent to which the protection of jursdiction is pursued, and the nature of the mechanisms used to accomplish it, vary greatly from government to government.

Intergovernmental affairs agencies are able to to monitor the panorama of policy sectors in order to detect intrusions by other governments. Moreover, they can maintain a qualified source of expertise in order to support jurisdictional battles. They also provide a locus where constitutional research and expertise can be concentrated, thereby assisting a government in the defense of its jurisdiction, whether in the courts or in political negotiations.

Related to the broad goal of jurisdictional protection are more specific goals that a government might have with respect to constitutional developments. In constitutional talks, for the most part, governments hope to either maintain the *status quo* or to enhance their areas of jurisdiction.

Intergovernmental affairs agencies have played a key role in constitutional negotiations for several reasons. First, the scope of discussions has been so broad that in order to obtain a coordinated "government" position, an agency separate from the various departmental views was required. Moreover, because of its importance, many first ministers wanted constitutional reform to be handled by a unit that was close to them. Intergovernmental agencies necessarily have close links with the premier or prime minister.

Government objectives in constitutional reform relate to defending jurisdiction, an area where some intergovernmental affairs agencies have developed expertise. Lastly, the constitutional reform process was a negotiating process with very high stakes. As was noted above officials in intergovernmental agencies are very capable in negotiating techniques and in reaching agreements and accords.

Some analysts have suggested that the only real importance of intergovernmental affairs agencies has been their role with respect to the constitution. It is implied that perhaps the intergovernmental objectives of governments have changed over time. During the era of constitutional negotiations, it was necessary for governments to have a central agency concentrating on constitutional matters and developing the expertise to enable the government to defend or enhance its jurisdiction from the best possible position. Since 1982, so the argument goes, the usefulness of this sort of agency has been outlived.

While it is true that the constitutional issue greatly enhanced the role and influence of intergovernmental agencies, and in some cases was a key factor in determining the structural arrangements within an agency, no intergovernmental affairs agency was created solely because of this issue. In virtually all governments, there was some specialized intergovernmental unit in existence prior to the major wave of constitutional negotiations (1978-1981). If there were a single factor that spurred on the creation of central agencies for intergovernmental affairs, it is more likely that it was the tremendous growth in interaction among governments generally, and in the use of the shared-cost agreement during the 1960s and early 1970s specifically, rather than the rise of the constitutional issue.

Conclusion
It is clear that there are some functions performed exclusively by intergovernmental affairs agencies which

serve to assist governments in reaching some of their objectives. It is also apparent that intergovernmental affairs agencies can play a useful role regardless of the key issues on the public agenda at any point in time. The value of these agencies is not restricted to certain periods – such as during constitutional negotiations or when highly conflictual issues are being discussed at the political level.

In recent years, some intergovernmental agencies have shown an ability to adapt to the changing priorities of their governments by assuming a key role in their government's international relations. This role has been heightened as preparations for negotiating a new trade arrangement with the United States begin. Some intergovernmental affairs agencies will play a major role in formulating their government's policy on this issue.

Why is there this "persistence" in intergovernmental affairs agencies? Interdependence among governments is a fundamental fact of policy-making in Canada. Because of their reliance on other governments, all governments face a high level of uncertainty. Specialized agencies were created in response to this uncertainty. Through their capacity to coordinate interaction with other governments in all sectors, through their contacts and lines of communication with other governments, and through their abilities in developing strategy and negotiating, intergovernmental affairs agencies have helped governments to reduce the uncertainty and to "manage" the interface.

What is the future of intergovernmental affairs agencies? While there can only be speculation about the answer, it seems likely that the nature, the size, and the functions of these agencies throughout governments in Canada will continue to vary and to evolve. As long as interdependence underlies Canadian federalism, however, there will exist a need for such agencies to help governments deal with the resulting uncertainty.

Notes

1. Government of Manitoba. *Report of the Task Force on Government Organization and Economy*, 31 March 1978, pp. 93-4.
2. Government of Manitoba, p. 94.
3. Timothy Woolstencroft, *Organizing Intergovernmental Relations*. Kingston: Institute of Intergovernmental Relations, 1982, p. 76.
4. Howard Leeson, "Accommodative Mechanisms in a Decentralizing Federation: The Intergovernmental Affairs Function in Saskatchewan." Presented to the Institute for Public Administration, St. John's, 30 August 1985, pp. 1-2.
5. Department of Finance, *The Fiscal Plan*, May 1985, p.27.

APPENDIX:
PROFILES OF INTERGOVERNMENTAL AFFAIRS AGENCIES IN CANADA

The subsequent pages contain a series of profiles that describe the key intergovernmental affairs agency in each of the 13 governments (federal, provincial, and territorial) in Canada. Each profile summarizes the evolution of the agency, its statutory base (where one exists), its financial and personnel resources, external offices for which it is responsible, and its mandate.

Information for these profiles was gleaned from a variety of sources, including annual reports, brochures, internal documents, organizational tables, and interviews with officials. A draft copy of each profile was sent to an official in the relevant agency for his or her comments; these were subsequently integrated into the final version.

Certain qualifications must be made. With respect to the financial figures, either public accounts data or budgetary estimates have been used, depending on their availability. An effort was made to be consistent. Sources for all data are listed.

Although the organizational charts for some of the agencies are reproduced from public documents, for other agencies they have been created on the basis of interviews and descriptive survey. As a result, while every effort has been made to create charts which accurately reflect the relationships among various components within an agency, the tables in the following profiles are not official.

Each profile also includes a list of formal intergovernmental affairs units which exist in some of the sectoral departments within the government. It must be acknowledged that there are units in other departments which are involved in intergovernmental policy-making, but are excluded here because that is not their primary focus. Moreover, in some government departments, there are individuals working on a full-time basis with intergovernmental issues. However, because they are in a unit with broader planning or policy-making responsibilities, they are also excluded here.

CANADA

Federal-Provincial Relations Office

1985 ORGANIZATION

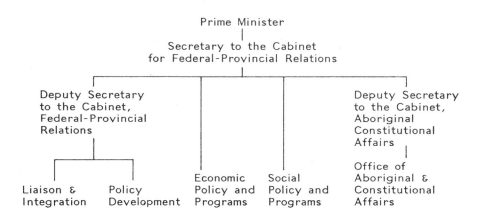

Prime Minister

Secretary to the Cabinet
for Federal-Provincial Relations

Deputy Secretary to the Cabinet, Federal-Provincial Relations		Economic Policy and Programs	Social Policy and Programs	Deputy Secretary to the Cabinet, Aboriginal Constitutional Affairs
Liaison & Integration	Policy Development			Office of Aboriginal & Constitutional Affairs

HISTORY

The Federal-Provincial Relations Secretariat (FPRS) was established in 1968 as part of the Privy Council Office to coordinate the federal government's relations with provincial governments; to ensure the coordinated implementation of the government's policy on bilingualism in the public service; to oversee constitutional review; and to coordinate federal government plans for the National Capital. The Secretariat was established in conjunction with the Cabinet Committee on Federal-Provincial Relations in 1968. In 1977, that committee's responsibilities were assumed by the Cabinet Committee on Planning and Priorities.

The Federal-Provincial Relations Office (FPRO), which evolved from the FPRS, was established by an Act respecting the office of the Secretary to the Cabinet for Federal-Provincial Relations and came into being as a separate entity on January 15, 1975. On February 4, 1975, a regulation (P.C. 1975-250) was passed, designating the "Federal-Provincial Relations Office as a Department, Prime Minister as Appropriate Minister and Secretary to the Cabinet for Federal-Provincial Relations as Deputy Head." From 1977 until 1980, there was a Minister of State for Federal-Provincial Relations in the federal cabinet.

Throughout the years, the FPRO has undergone several internal reorganizations, although its basic purpose and mandate remain largely unchanged. For the most part, the changes in organization have reflected changes on the intergovernmental agenda. In the mid-1970s, the FPRO was divided into three sections, each headed by an assistant secretary: Regional Analysis, Policy and Program Review, and Studies and Research. A constitutional advisor was on staff and a Deputy Secretary to the Cabinet was responsible for co-ordination of national unity questions.

In the late 1970s, a reorganization of the FPRO created two Deputy Secretaries to the Cabinet, one for Federal-Provincial Relations and one for the Renewal of Federalism. Three sections existed, each headed by an Assistant Secretary to Cabinet: Operations; Planning, Analysis, and Research; and Constitutional Review.

Following the appointment of Michael Kirby as Secretary to the Cabinet for Federal-Provincial Relations in 1980, the FPRO was restructured. Four branches, each directed by an Assistant Secretary, were established: Strategic Planning, Liaison, Economic Policy and Programs, and Social Policy and Programs.

Further minor changes were made to the organization during 1982 and 1983. Currently, the FPRO is composed of five sections, each headed by an Assistant Secretary to Cabinet: Policy Development; Liaison and Integration; Economic Policy and Programs; Social Policy and Programs; and the Office of Aboriginal Constitutional Affairs (OACA). The Assistant Secretaries for Policy Development and for Liaison and Integration report to a Deputy Secretary for Federal-Provincial Relations. There is also a Deputy Secretary for Aboriginal Constitutional Affairs, to whom OACA reports.

STATUTES

An Act respecting the Office of the Secretary to the Cabinet for Federal-Provincial Relations and respecting the Clerk of the Privy Council
(Statutes of Canada, 1974-75-76, chapter 16)
This act amended various Acts related to public service employment to provide for the position of the Secretary to the Cabinet for Federal-Provincial Relations and the Federal-Provincial Relations Office (FPRO).

MANDATE

The objectives of the FPRO, as outlined by Prime Minister Trudeau in December 1974, are: to advise and assist the Prime Minister in his overall responsibility for federal-provincial relations; to provide Cabinet with greater assistance in examining federal-provincial issues of current and long-term concern; to promote and facilitate federal-provincial cooperation and consultation; and to assist federal departments whenever they deal with provincial ministers and their agencies.[1]

The FPRO provides a coordinating and advisory function on behalf of the Government of Canada as a whole. It provides a link among the Prime Minister, the cabinet and individual departments, as well as the provincial governments.

The FPRO has responsibility for the assessment of federal-provincial aspects of social and economic policy. It has the lead role in strategic planning in the federal-provincial and constitutional realms and is the principal agency responsible for advising the government on federal-provincial and constitutional matters. The FPRO assists line departments in their relations with provincial governments. It is responsible for coordinating preparations for First Ministers' Conferences.

The organization of the FPRO was revised during 1982 and 1983. The current structure is as follows:

- The Social and Economic Policy Secretariats ensure that a federal-provincial perspective is brought to bear on the development of social and economic policies.

- The Policy Development Secretariat formulates recommendations on constitutional change, except that concerning aboriginal people, and reform of governmental institutions. It is responsible for developing advice on the government's overall approach to federal-provincial relations.

- The Integration and Liaison Secretariat monitors and analyzes issues in federal-provincial relations and events in provincial affairs.

- The Office of Aboriginal Constitutional Affairs was established by the Prime Minister following the March 1983 First Ministers' Conference on Aboriginal Constitutional Matters. It acts as a central policy and coordinating unit for the ongoing process aimed at resolving constitutional issues affecting aboriginal peoples.

RESOURCES

Financial[2]

Federal-Provincial Relations Office

	Expenditure (Estimates)
1974-75	1,127,000
1975-76	1,464,000
1976-77	1,800,000
1977-78	2,012,000
1978-79	3,810,000
1979-80	3,498,000
1980-81	3,984,000
1981-82	4,340,000
1982-83	4,429,000
1983-84	4,794,000
1984-85	4,198,000
1985-86	4,747,000

Personnel[3]

	Person-Years (Estimates)
1974-75	52

116

1975-76	57
1976-77	60
1977-78	60
1978-79	82
1979-80	82
1980-81	87
1981-82	78
1982-83	65
1983-84	75
1984-85	59
1985-86	64

INTERGOVERNMENTAL UNITS IN OTHER DEPARTMENTS

Department of Communications
    Federal-Provincial Relations

Employment and Immigration Canada
    Intergovernmental Affairs and External Liaison

Department of Energy, Mines and Resources
    Federal-Provincial and Territorial Energy Relations
    Division

Department of the Environment
    Intergovernmental Affairs Directorate

Department of Finance
    Federal-Provincial Relations and Social Policy Branch

Department of Fisheries and Oceans
    Federal-Provincial Relations Division

Health and Welfare Canada
    Intergovernmental and International Affairs Branch

Department of Indian Affairs and Northern Development
    Intergovernmental Affairs Directorate

Department of Labour
    Policy and Liaison, Federal-Provincial Relations
    Branch

Revenue Canada (Taxation)
   Legislation Branch, Provincial and International
   Relations Division

Department of Transport
   Intergovernmental and Industrial Relations Division

Notes

1. *House of Commons Debates and Proceedings*, December 18, 1974, p. 2364.
2. Government of Canada, *Main Estimates*, various years.
3. *Ibid*.

ALBERTA

Department of Federal and Intergovernmental Affairs

1985 ORGANIZATION

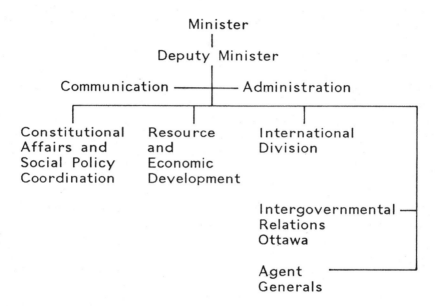

HISTORY

The first Federal and Intergovernmental Affairs Minister was appointed in 1971, although the Department of Federal and Intergovernmental Affairs (FIGA) was not established until June 1972. It evolved from a unit which had been established by the previous administration in the Executive Council Office.

In the 13-year history of the Department, there have been a number of organizational changes. Initially, FIGA was divided into three functional categories: Resources and Industrial Development; Social and Cultural Affairs; and Constitutional and Economic Affairs. In 1974, a Research and Planning Division was created, and the functions of the Constitutional and Economic Affairs Division were distributed among the other three

Divisions. An Urban Affairs and Housing Division was created in 1977.

In the spring of 1978, the Department was reorganized into four divisions: Resources and Industrial Development (later changed to Resources and Economic Development), Social and Cultural Affairs, Research and Planning, and a new International Division. In 1985, the Research and Planning Division was amalgamated with Social and Cultural Affairs to become "Constitutional Affairs and Social Policy Coordination".

In December 1982, a Communications Director was assigned to the Department. She is responsible for all public relations and information functions within the Department, and acts in an advisory and coordinating role for out-of-province and foreign offices.

STATUTES

The Department of Federal and Intergovernmental Affairs Act, 1972
This Act provided for the creation of the Department of Federal and Intergovernmental Affairs (FIGA), over which a Minister of the Executive Council presides. The Minister is responsible for the coordination of all policies, programs and activities of the Government of Alberta in relation to other governments. He is to conduct a continuing review of all such policies and activities of the Government of Alberta. He is to be a party to the negotiation of all proposed intergovernmental agreements. As well, he may establish and maintain offices outside of Alberta for the purpose of initiating or maintaining intergovernmental cooperation.

According to the Act, an intergovernmental agreement must be signed on behalf of the Government by the Minister of FIGA, either alone or with another Minister of the Crown, or be approved by the Minister of FIGA, depending on the nature of the agreement and the regulations governing it.

The Lieutenant Governor in Council may make regulations designating the classes of intergovernmental agreements to be signed by the Minister of Federal and

Intergovernmental Affairs only, or by other ministers as well.

The Statutes Amendment (Grant Provisions) Act, 1977
This Act provided for, among other things, an amendment to *The Department of Federal and Intergovernmental Affairs Act,* authorizing the Minister to make grants in cases where he is so authorized.

MANDATE

In 1971, it was recognized that a separate department which could direct its full attention to intergovernmental affairs was needed. Donald Getty, the first minister of the Department of Federal and Intergovernmental Affairs (FIGA), pointed out in 1972 that in the past, contacts between the Government of Alberta and other governments had often been uncoordinated and, at times, conflicting. Not only did this create confusion for the other governments, the federal government was able to use the lack of coordination and policy in intergovernmental matters to "out-manoeuvre" the province. [1]
    A small unit for intergovernmental affairs had been created in the Executive Council Office by the previous government. Donald Getty stated that this agency had no control or authority and was, for the most part, ignored by the rest of the government. [2] Mr. Getty argued that intergovernmental matters were too important for such an agency – they must be the responsibility of an elected cabinet minister.
    For these reasons, an intergovernmental affairs department, under the direction of a senior cabinet minister and having substantial mechanisms of control, was created. The new department, FIGA, was to be primarily responsible for the coordination of policies, programs and activities of the Government of Alberta in relation to other governments.
    The administration of programs and the articulation of specific policy positions, for the most part, remains within other departments. However, it is the responsibility of FIGA "to ensure coordination,

consistency and continuity in government policies when other governments are involved."[3] FIGA was given responsibility for representing Alberta's interests as an equal partner in Confederation and ensuring that all activities of the Alberta government in relation to the federal, territorial, other provincial governments, and governments of foreign countries or states are conducted in a coordinated and consistent manner.

FIGA is comprised of three divisions. Together, these are responsible for the intergovernmental aspects in the entire spectrum of sectors in which the Government of Alberta is involved. The Resources and Economic Development Division is responsible for issues relating to natural resource ownership and development, energy, economic development, transportation, agriculture, communications, environment, consumer and corporate affairs, tourism and small business and regional economic development.

The International Division is responsible for monitoring and coordinating Alberta's international activities, and for reviewing provincial policies and programs in relation to Canada's foreign policy and that of other countries.

The newly-formed Constitutional Affairs and Social Policy Coordination Division is responsible for the intergovernmental aspects of issues having a social or cultural dimension. Moreover, it has responsibility for "providing an ongoing assessment of federal-provincial and interprovincial relations and the institutions of federalism."[4] Specifically, it is responsible for matters such as constitutional affairs, fiscal and economic relations, Senate reform, and the reduction of federal-provincial duplication.

RESOURCES

Financial[5]

	Expenditure
1970-71	33,802
1971-72	156,852
1972-73	320,001
1974-75	982,250

1975-76	1,700,884
1976-77	1,615,770
1977-78	2,172,618
1978-79	2,396,178
1979-80	2,597,619
1980-81	3,547,960
1981-82	4,526,870
1982-83	5,029,694
1983-84	5,558,659
1984-85	6,018,982*
1985-86	6,346,806*

Personnel[6]

	Full-time Employees
1975-76	56
1976-77	47
1979-80	59
1980-81	61
1981-82	64
1982-83	66
1984-85	67
1985-86	67*

*Estimates

EXTERNAL OFFICES

Ottawa
The Ottawa Office has existed since the early 1930s. Since 1972, it has been under the auspices of FIGA. Its main purpose is to act as a "listening post" for the Alberta Government. It is also involved in making administrative arrangements for First Ministers' Conferences and in answering enquiries regarding manpower requirements and business opportunities in Alberta.

International Offices
The following offices are administered by FIGA and are each directed by an Agent General.

London: dates from 1925; transferred to FIGA in
1973.
Tokyo: opened in 1970 and transferred to FIGA in
1972.
Hong Kong: opened in 1980.
New York: opened in 1982.

The Alberta Government also has offices in Los Angeles
and Houston. These are the responsibility of the Alberta
Economic Development Department.

INTERGOVERNMENTAL UNITS IN OTHER DEPARTMENTS

Department of Social Services and Community Health
Federal-Provincial Coordination

Department of Treasury
Fiscal Policy and Economic Analysis

Department of Energy and Natural Resources
Director of Government Relations (Ottawa)

Notes

1. *Alberta Hansard*, March 10, 1972, pp. 7-22.
2. *Ibid*, pp. 7-25.
3. *Annual Report Number 10*, Department of Federal and
   Intergovernmental Affairs, 1982-83, p. 6.
4. *Ibid*, p. 7.
5. 1970-71 to 1983-84: *Public Accounts*, various years.
   1984-85 to 1985-86: *Alberta Government Estimates*,
   various years.
6. 1975-76 to 1984-85: *Public Service Commissioner
   Annual Report*, Alberta Personnel Administration,
   various years.
   1985-86: *Alberta Government Estimates, 1985-86*.

BRITISH COLUMBIA

Ministry of Intergovernmental Relations

1985 ORGANIZATION

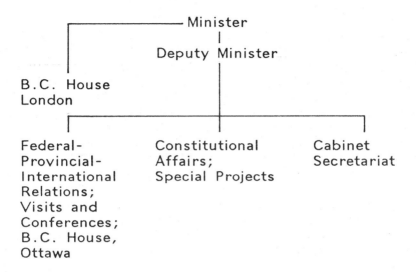

HISTORY

In 1975, a department in the Office of the Premier was created to hold responsibility for the government's intergovernmental relations, executive council administration and reform of the Constitution. On November 23, 1979, the Ministry of Intergovernmental Relations was formed to take over these responsibilities. There are currently five main units in the Ministry:

1. Federal-Provincial Relations
2. Constitutional Affairs and Special Projects
3. Official Visits and Conferences
4. Cabinet Secretariat
5. B.C. House, London

STATUTES

Constitution Act (OIC 2957), 1979
This Act established, among others, the Ministry of Intergovernmental Relations.

Constitution Act (OIC 2988), 1979
This Act concerned ministerial functions for various ministries. The Minister of Intergovernmental Relations was charged with the administration of the Agent-General's office and British Columbia House in London, England, and the office of Intergovernmental Relations and Executive Council.

Ministry of Intergovernmental Relations Act, 1980
This Act provided for the creation of the Ministry of Intergovernmental Relations and for a Minister to preside over it. The mandate of the Ministry is:

- to coordinate the activities of, to make recommendations to and to develop programs and policies for the Executive Council in relation to federal-provincial, interprovincial, and extraprovincial affairs; and
- to act as secretariat to the Executive Council and its committees and to coordinate policy development among the Ministries.

According to the Act, the Minister may, on behalf of the Government, enter into agreements with other governments.[1]

MANDATE

When the Ministry of Intergovernmental Relations was created in 1979, a reference paper was released, outlining its purposes and functions. According to this paper, the new Ministry was: to coordinate and develop policies, strategies and activities regarding British Columbia's relations with other governments; to coordinate and develop the province's policy on proposals to reform federalism; to facilitate the functioning of the

Cabinet committee system; to ensure adequate consultation and coordination regarding all submissions to Executive Council; to advise the Premier on the allocation of responsibilities to Cabinet committees and Ministries.[2] It was to review all submissions to Executive Council committees and Treasury Board to determine whether Ministries with an interest in a submission have been adequately consulted by the sponsoring ministry.

Following is a summary of the three main Divisions in the Ministry:[3]

Constitutional Affairs and Special Projects Division
This Division monitors all federal-provincial developments affecting constitutional and jurisdictional issues. It advises, briefs and represents the B.C. government in relevant discussions. Aboriginal constitutional reform has been one of its major concerns in recent years. Other issues include property rights, senate reform, administrative tribunals, and offshore resources.

Federal-Provincial-International Relations Division
This basic objective of the Division is to ensure that British Columbia's relations with the federal government, the governments of other provinces, and the governments of other countries are conducted in a consistent, coordinated, and effective manner. This involves coordinating British Columbia's overall approach to intergovernmental relations; monitoring activities of the federal, provincial and foreign governments, and the possible effects of these activities on provincial affairs; and keeping all line Ministries informed of current developments in other jurisdictions.

The Visit and Conferences Branch coordinates visits from Canadian and foreign representatives, assists in the planning and briefing of foreign visits by government ministers and officials, and provides logistical support for major conferences and events in which the Province participates.

Cabinet Secretariat
The Cabinet Secretariat is responsible for providing administrative support to the Cabinet and all its

committees, including three standing committees, three management and coordinating committees, and four special committees. The last category includes a Cabinet Committee on Federal-Provincial Relations, which is chaired by the Minister of Intergovernmental Relations.

RESOURCES

Financial[4]
Office of Intergovernmental Relations,
in Executive Council Office

	Expenditure
1976-77	290,145
1978-79	243,591
1979-80	299,194

Ministry of Intergovernmental Relations

1979-80	137,719
1980-81	2,089,051
1981-82	2,448,616
1982-83	2,472,450
1983-84	2,069,757
1984-85	2,435,407*
1985-86	2,631,778*

Personnel[5]
Office of Intergovernmental Relations,
in Executive Council Office

	Employees
1978-79	10
1979-80	9

Ministry of Intergovernmental Relations

as of:	Employees
Dec 31, 1980	24
Dec 31, 1981	32
Mar 31, 1982	40
Mar 31, 1983	48
1983-84	47*
1984-85	40*
1985-86	42*

*Estimates

EXTERNAL OFFICES

Ottawa
Opened in 1980, B.C. House in the nation's capital serves as "a communications and information conduit" between B.C. and the federal government.[6] It monitors federal policy and legislative initiatives and provides administrative support for Ministers and officials attending meetings in Ottawa. The B.C. House representative may attend meetings or conferences on behalf of the Ministry or other line Ministries. B.C. House also serves a tourist information function for the province.

London, England
British Columbia's first Agent General in London was appointed in 1872. B.C. House represents an important presence for the province in the United Kingdom and Europe. Among its functions are: promoting B.C. products and interests in the U.K. and Europe; arranging itineraries for provincial Ministers, officials, and business and culture groups visiting Europe; and welcoming British Columbians travelling in Europe.

INTERGOVERNMENTAL UNITS IN OTHER DEPARTMENTS

Ministry of Finance
Taxation and Intergovernmental Relations Branch, Treasury Board

Ministry of Labour
Federal-Provincial Relations, Labour Market Branch

Notes

1. Section 4.
2. *Annual Report 1979 to 1981*, Ministry of Intergovernmental Relations, 1982 pp. 12-14.
3. from *Annual Report* April 1, 1983 to March 31, 1984, Ministry of Intergovernmental Relations.
4. 1976-77 to 1983-84: *Public Accounts*, various years.

1984-85 to 1985-86: *Estimates,* various years.

5.   1978-79 to 1979-1980: *Estimates,* various years. 1980-1983: "Total Employees Paid", *Annual Report,* Public Service Commission, various years. 1983-84 to 1985-86: "Full-time Equivalent Employees", *Estimates,* various years.

MANITOBA

Federal Provincial Relations Secretariat,
Executive Council Office

1985 ORGANIZATION

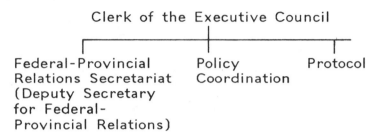

Executive Council Office

Clerk of the Executive Council

Federal-Provincial   Policy   Protocol
Relations Secretariat   Coordination
(Deputy Secretary
for Federal-
Provincial Relations)

HISTORY

Since 1942, the Premier of Manitoba has assumed the title
of Minister of Dominion-Provincial Relations
(Federal-Provincial Relations since 1980). At the
administrative level, the Clerk of the Executive Council
has historically been active in directing
intergovernmental policy. Until 1983, however, there was
no separate unit in the Executive Council Office that was
specifically responsible for intergovernmental affairs.
Since the late 1950s, the Federal-Provincial Relations and
Research Division in the Department of Finance was the
government's principal agency in this regard.
     In 1983, a small Federal-Provincial Relations
Secretariat was created in the Executive Council Office.
It assumed responsibility for non-financial aspects of
intergovernmental relations. The Secretariat is headed
by a Deputy Secretary to the Cabinet for
Federal-Provincial Relations.

MANDATE

For many years, federal-provincial relations have been
the responsibility of the first minister. The Premier has

131

been nominally the Minister responsible for this field for a longer period than in any other jurisdiction. However, throughout the 1960s and 1970s, it was the Federal-Provincial Relations and Research Division in the Department of Finance that was the principal agency in the government responsible for intergovernmental affairs.

The Federal-Provincial Relations and Research Division was responsible for the Finance Department's activities with respect to federal-provincial financial and economic matters and for providing assistance on a continuing basis to ministers of other departments on a broad range of intergovernmental issues. In this capacity, the Division provided research and other advisory services to numerous ministers and senior officials with respect to issues where departments other than Finance had the lead responsibility in federal-provincial negotiations.

The functions of this Division included:

- economic policy analysis and research;
- federal-provincial economic analysis;
- federal-provincial relations, involving research and analysis of intergovernmental endeavours, and the research and coordination of various conferences and negotiations;
- shared-cost program analysis; and
- administration of federal-provincial fiscal arrangements.

The Report of the Task Force on Government Organization and Economy (TFOGE), which reported to the Manitoba government in 1978, noted that there was:

> no identifiable group within government whose function it is to offer comprehensive advice on federal-provincial issues and strategies....[There was] no reliable mechanism...through which one could obtain a comprehensive view and through which one could evaluate what is happening, week by week, through the whole of the system.[1]

The 1978 Report recommended that a small group be created in the Office of the Executive Council to advise the Premier on federal-provincial and interprovincial policy issues and constitutional matters. [2]

In 1983, a Federal-Provincial Relations Secretariat was created in the Executive Council Office. It assumed responsibility for coordinating some of the non-financial intergovernmental issues with which the Federal-Provincial Relations and Research Division in the Finance Department had been involved. The bulk of its work is directly for the Premier, involving preparation for First Ministers' and Premiers' Conferences. It is also responsible for Manitoba's regional development agreements with the federal government. The Clerk of the Executive Council is responsible for coordinating Manitoba's subsidiary agreements reached under its umbrella Economic and Regional Development Agreement (ERDA) with the federal government. The Federal-Provincial Relations Secretariat in the Executive Council Office remains small and, as a result, is limited in the extent to which it can provide a comprehensive approach to intergovernmental policy.

RESOURCES[3]

Financial
Federal-Provincial Relations Secretariat,
Executive Council Office
    1984-85   169,400

Personnel
    1985   4

INTERGOVERNMENTAL UNITS IN OTHER DEPARTMENTS

Department of Finance
    Federal-Provincial Relations and Research Division
    1985-86 Budget: 1,099,800

Department of Agriculture
    Coordinator of Federal-Provincial Agreements

Department of Employment Services and Economic
Security
   Federal-Provincial   Programs   Coordination   Branch
   (Employment Services Division)

Notes

1.   *Report of the Task Force on Government Organization
     and Economy*, Volume 1, 1978, pp. 95-6.
2.   *Ibid.*, p. 64.
3.   *Main Estimates*, 1985-86, p. 8.

NEW BRUNSWICK

Intergovernmental Affairs, Cabinet Secretariat

1985 ORGANIZATION

Cabinet Secretariat

Chief of Protocol	Chairman of Cabinet Secretariat	Intergovernmental Affairs and Legislation (Deputy Minister)

Secretary to Cabinet Committee on Social Development	Secretary to Cabinet Committee on Economic Development

HISTORY

The Cabinet Secretariat was created as part of the Premier's Office in 1971. It has the duty of providing administrative support and policy advice to the Cabinet and to various committees of Cabinet.[1] Currently, there are three Cabinet committees: the Committee on Economic Development, the Committee on Social Development, and the Executive Committee of Cabinet. All three are to some extent concerned with intergovernmental aspects of policy.

The Cabinet Committees on Social Development and Economic Development were created in November 1974. Each is served by staffs located in the Cabinet Secretariat under the direction of their respective Deputy Secretaries to Cabinet. Their responsibilities include the intergovernmental aspects related to the social and economic development policy areas.

The Executive Committee of Cabinet was established in 1983. It is chaired by the Premier and is served by the Chairman of the Cabinet Secretariat who acts as

Secretary to the Committee. It replaced the Policy and Priorities Committee of Cabinet which had existed throughout the 1970s. Part of that body's mandate required that it review and recommend to the Cabinet legislative amendments to be proposed to the Legislative Assembly. It advised the Premier and Cabinet regarding intergovernmental relations.[2] It was served by a small intergovernmental affairs unit.

Currently, there is an Intergovernmental Affairs and Legislation unit in the Cabinet Secretariat. It is headed by a Deputy Minister and includes two officers. The Deputy Minister is responsible for advising the Executive Committee of Cabinet on intergovernmental policy. As well, he chairs the only committee of deputy ministers within the Cabinet Secretariat: the Officials' Committee of the Executive Council.

MANDATE

Much of the work of the Intergovernmental Affairs and Legislation unit in the Cabinet Secretariat involves preparation for meetings and conferences involving the Premier. The agency intercedes in issues when affairs are not functioning smoothly, when significant new departures are embarked upon, or when the involvement of the most senior level of government is required. No attempt is made to monitor intergovernmental issues on a comprehensive basis. This unit has played a key role in determining the New Brunswick government's position on constitutional issues. Currently, it assumes responsibility for policies with respect to aboriginal matters. Until recently, it handled protocol duties; these are now the responsibility of a separate unit within the Cabinet Secretariat.

Other units are also involved in intergovernmental issues. For example, the Secretary to the Cabinet Committee on Economic Development is responsible for coordinating the Province's regional development agreements signed with the federal government under its umbrella Economic and Regional Development Agreement (ERDA).

RESOURCES

Financial[3]
Cabinet Secretariat
(Note: resources for the intergovernmental affairs
        function are not separated.)

	Expenditure
1979-80	1,136,277
1980-81	1,477,865
1981-82	1,388,663
1982-83	1,165,346
1983-84	951,629

INTERGOVERNMENTAL UNITS IN OTHER DEPARTMENTS

Department of Finance
   Taxation and Fiscal Policy

Department of Social Services
   Communications and Federal-Provincial Relations

Notes

1. *The Estimates, 1983-84*, p. 58.
2. *Ibid.*
3. *Public Accounts*, various years.

NEWFOUNDLAND

Intergovernmental Affairs Secretariat

1985 ORGANIZATION

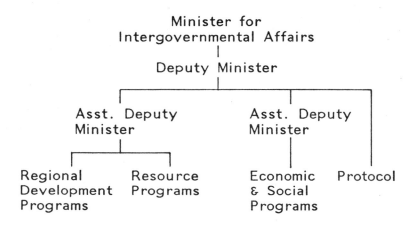

HISTORY

In 1974, there was established in the Planning and Priorities Committee Secretariat a Director of Intergovernmental Relations. One year later, the Secretariat for Intergovernmental Affairs was created. It was part of a major reorganization of the Executive Council Office, wherein three secretariats were formed: the Cabinet Secretariat; the Treasury Board Secretariat; and the Intergovernmental Affairs Secretariat.

From 1980 to 1982, the Intergovernmental Affairs Secretariat assumed responsibility for communications. That division is currently part of a new Department of Consumer Affairs and Communications.

The Intergovernmental Affairs Secretariat has four divisions: Regional Development Programs; Resource Programs; Economic and Social Programs; and Protocol.

STATUTES

An Act to Provide for the Direction of Intergovernmental Affairs in the Province, 1975
This Act provided for the establishment of an Intergovernmental Affairs Secretariat to be operated under the direction of a Minister of the Crown, and the appointment of an Executive Director who would have the powers of a deputy head of a department.

The Minister is responsible for the coordination of all policies, programs and activities of the government in relation to any sovereign government. As well, he is to review on a continuous basis all such policies, all intergovernmental agreements, and all relevant legislation. He is to be a party to the negotiation of all proposed intergovernmental agreements.

The Act compels every intergovernmental agreement, prior to its execution, to be signed by the Minister of Intergovernmental Affairs, as well as by the Minister administering the Department to which the agreement relates, or else the agreement is not binding on the province.

The Government Reorganization Act, 1981
Part VII of this Act revised the 1975 *Intergovernmental Affairs Act*. It replaced the section concerning the appointment of an Executive Director with a provision for the appointment of a Deputy Minister of Inter-governmental Affairs.

This Act also extended the powers of the Minister to include the supervision, control and direction of all matters within the legislative authority of the province relating to communications. This section has since been rescinded.

MANDATE

The Intergovernmental Affairs Secretariat is responsible, in conjunction with the line departments, for all intergovernmental matters, including federal-provincial and interprovincial agreements.[1] Under the terms of the 1975 statute, the Minister of Intergovernmental Affairs has extensive authority in this area, such that all intergovernmental agreements must be signed by him in order to be legally binding.

The Secretariat is organized so that it is able to coordinate and monitor intergovernmental activity in virtually every sector. The Economic and Social Programs Division and the Resource Programs Division monitor activities in their respective fields.

The Regional Development Programs Division is responsible for the coordination of negotiations and overseeing the implementation of all cost-shared agreements and subsidiary agreements signed with the federal government under the umbrella Economic and Regional Development Agreement (ERDA).

Finally, the Protocol Division is responsible for the coordination of all aspects related to diplomatic visits to the Province.

RESOURCES

Financial[2]

	Expenditure
1974-75	230,900
1975-76	329,030
1976-77	403,673
1977-78	468,625
1978-79	563,556
1980-81	690,084
1981-82	1,096,868
1982-83	1,452,201
1983-84	1,438,148
1984-85	2,075,700*

*Estimate

Personnel[3]

	Permanent Employees (Estimates)
1975-76	18
1976-77	19
1977-78	23
1978-79	24
1979-80	24
1980-81	23
1981-82	26
1982-83	32
1983-84	33
1984-85	33
1985-86	26

INTERGOVERNMENTAL UNITS IN OTHER DEPARTMENTS

Department of Finance
Federal-Provincial Fiscal Relations, Fiscal Policy Branch

Notes

1. *Estimates*, 1978-79, p. 12.
2. 1974-75 to 1983-84: *Public Accounts*, various years. 1984-85: *Estimates, 1984-85*.
3. *Salary Details, Revised Estimates*, various years.

NOVA SCOTIA

Policy Board Secretariat

1985 ORGANIZATION

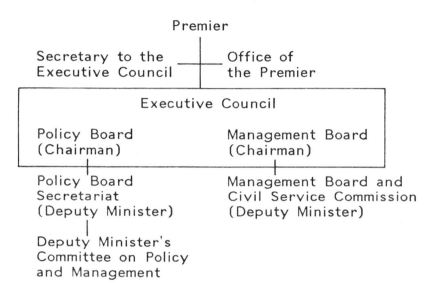

Premier

Secretary to the
Executive Council

Office of
the Premier

Executive Council

Policy Board
(Chairman)

Management Board
(Chairman)

Policy Board
Secretariat
(Deputy Minister)

Management Board and
Civil Service Commission
(Deputy Minister)

Deputy Minister's
Committee on Policy
and Management

HISTORY

An Office of Intergovernmental Affairs was created in 1979 as part of a general reform of the Executive Council Office. At the same time, two cabinet committees were also created: the Policy Board and the Management Board. Each board had its own secretariat, headed by a Deputy Minister. The Management Board is responsible for the internal operations of government, exercising essentially treasury board functions. The Policy Board was initially chaired by the Premier and was composed of eight other ministers. Its principal function is "to develop and recommend the policies and priorities for consideration by the Executive Council as a whole."[1]

Created in conjunction with the Policy Board was a permanent Deputy Ministers' Committee on Policy and Management, chaired by the Deputy Minister of Policy Board. The Committee provides all Deputy Ministers with an opportunity to discuss and advise on policy and management practices, and serves to link them directly with Cabinet and its committees.

From 1979 to 1982, a minister other than the Premier assumed responsibility for intergovernmental affairs. In 1982, the Premier assumed this role. The following year, the Policy Board assumed responsibility for intergovernmental affairs and the Intergovernmental Affairs Office was disbanded. Its duties and staff were assigned to the Policy Board Secretariat. A 1985 reorganization created a separate cabinet position for the Chairman of Policy Board. The Premier, however, maintains responsibility for intergovernmental affairs.

BASIS

The Intergovernmental Affairs Office, which existed from 1979 until 1983, was created by order-in-council 79-141 – "Regulation Made by the Governor in Council Pursuant to the Public Service Act" – on February 13, 1979. The Office was to administer matters relating to intergovernmental affairs, forming part of the Executive Council Office. It was to be under the supervision, direction and control of the Minister of Intergovernmental Affairs.

Its duties, as laid out in the regulations, were:

- to act as a central coordinating agency for the Executive Council in the field of intergovernmental affairs;
- to undertake such studies relating to administrative or policy matters affecting relations with other jurisdictions as may be required by the Executive Council;
- to be informed as to pertinent administrative and policy matters in other jurisdictions.

MANDATE

The Office of Intergovernmental Affairs, created in 1979 and disbanded in 1983, was responsible for coordinating and evaluating federal-provincial and interprovincial relations, and acted as a resource centre on intergovernmental relations.

At the time of its inception, the purpose of the Office was to allow the government to plan and maximize its economic and fiscal relations with Ottawa, and with other governments. It was felt that because of its previous "piecemeal approach to federal assistance programs", Nova Scotia had missed opportunities to take full advantage of these programs.[2] As well, it was felt that Nova Scotia had suffered in terms of information exchange with other governments.

The main reason for the creation of the office was "to maintain and develop contacts and information which will allow it to evaluate, determine and act when the good of this province can be served."[3] During its existence, the Office worked extensively on Nova Scotia's position on constitutional negotiations.

The 1983 decision to disband the Office of Intergovernmental Affairs came in part because the constitutional issues no longer dominated the government's agenda. It was felt that there was no longer a need for a separate office.[4] Instead, intergovernmental relations became one of several functions handled by the Policy Board and the Policy Board Secretariat.

Related to this is the fact that intergovernmental policy in Nova Scotia is handled almost completely in the line departments. One of the most important aspects of intergovernmental affairs in Nova Scotia is federal-provincial agreements in the area of regional development. These are coordinated by the Department of Development. In large part, this department acts as a central agency for intergovernmental affairs, coordinating agreements and much of the interaction with other governments in the economic policy sectors.

RESOURCES

Financial[5]

Intergovernmental Affairs Office

	Expenditure
1979-80	57,217.95
1980-81	253,190.68
1981-82	292,758.32
1982-83	241,604.94

Policy Board

1983-84	642,706.64

Personnel[6]

Intergovernmental Affairs Office

	Employees
1978-79	6
as of:	
March 31, 1981	1
March 31, 1982	5
March 31, 1983	5

Policy Board

March 31, 1984	11

EXTERNAL OFFICE

Nova Scotia has an Agent General located in London, England. Although costs for the London office are included in the budget of the Department of Development, the Agent General generally reports directly to the Office of the Premier.

INTERGOVERNMENTAL UNITS IN OTHER DEPARTMENTS

Department of Finance
Federal-Provincial Taxation and Fiscal Relations Division.

Notes

1. Premier J. Buchanan, *Notes for Premier's News Conference on Government Reorganization*, 22 June 1979.
2. Nova Scotia. *House of Assembly Debates and Proceedings*. 6 April 1979, p. 1602.
3. *Ibid.*, p. 1603.
4. Interview.
5. Nova Scotia, *Public Accounts*, 1979-1984.
6. Nova Scotia Civil Service Commission, *Annual Reports*, 1979-1984.

ONTARIO

Ministry of Intergovernmental Affairs

1985 ORGANIZATION[1]

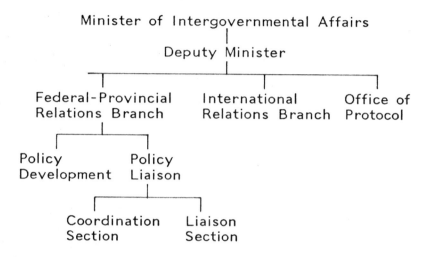

Minister of Intergovernmental Affairs

Deputy Minister

Federal-Provincial Relations Branch

International Relations Branch

Office of Protocol

Policy Development

Policy Liaison

Coordination Section

Liaison Section

HISTORY

The Department of Economics and Intergovernmental Relations was created in 1961 and briefly existed under Premier Leslie Frost. In 1965, Premier John Robarts established the Federal-Provincial and Interprovincial Affairs Secretariat.

In 1972, the Department of Treasury, Economics and Intergovernmental Affairs was established and six years later, in 1978, this department was split and a separate Ministry of Intergovernmental Affairs (MIA) created. It originally had responsibility for municipal affairs, but this was removed in 1981 when a separate Ministry of Municipal Affairs and Housing was created. Currently, the MIA is composed of a Federal-Provincial Relations Branch and an International Relations Branch. It also contains the Office of Protocol Services.

STATUTES

An Act to establish the Ministry of Treasury, Economics and Intergovernmental Affairs, 1972
The Act established the Ministry of Treasury, Economics and Intergovernmental Affairs, empowering the Treasurer of Ontario and Minister of Economics and Intergovernmental Affairs to recommend to the Executive Council financial, economic, accounting and taxation policy; advise on intergovernmental affairs; supervise, direct and control all financial, economic, statistical and accounting functions; and manage the Consolidated Revenue Fund and all public money.

An Act to establish the Ministry of Intergovernmental Affairs, 1978
This Act created the Ministry of Intergovernmental Affairs (MIA). It granted to the Minister responsibility for making recommendations to the Executive Council on the government's programs and activities in relation to federal-provincial, interprovincial and international affairs. It also granted to the Minister responsibility for the government's policies in relation to municipalities.

Amendment to 1978 Act, 1981
The main effect of the 1981 amendment was to remove responsibility for municipal affairs from the MIA.

MANDATE

The Ministry of Intergovernmental Affairs "performs essentially a co-ordinating and advisory function on behalf of the government as a whole."[2] Part of its mandate is to facilitate good working relationships with other governments, as well as "to defend the Province's interest within the framework of a strong, vigorous and united Canada."[3]

   The MIA has a unique role in Ontario, not being responsible for specific areas and programs, but rather providing a link between the Premier, the Cabinet and individual ministers, as well as with other governments and their representatives. The Ministry advises the

148

Premier and the Cabinet on overall policy and relations with other governments: it also assists other ministries on their specific intergovernmental policy issues or service needs.

The Federal-Provincial Relations Branch of the MIA seeks to ensure that the Ontario government speaks with a coordinated and effective voice in its dealings with other governments. In cooperation with other Ontario government ministries, its monitors developments in other provinces and in Ottawa. It aims to keep the Ontario government informed, to ensure that all ministries understand the relationship between their specific concerns and the broader issues; and to ensure that governments across Canada are aware of the policies and concerns of Ontario. Initially, this Branch was concerned almost exclusively with policy liaison: identifying, analyzing, and advising on the intergovernmental implications of policy and program initiatives in most sectors. However, in the early 1980s, this branch was divided into a Policy Liaison section and a Policy Development section. The former continued much as the branch had previously. The latter, however, was responsible for analyzing and developing strategic proposals concerning structural and long term trends in intergovernmental relations, including constitutional and institutional reform. In 1985, a third section — responsible for coordination — was created.

The International Relations Branch provides information and analysis on Ontario's relations with governments outside Canada. It coordinates the province's international activities, ensuring consistent and coherent policies. As well, the Ministry is responsible for protocol services on behalf of the Government as a whole.

RESOURCES

Financial[4]
Department of Treasury and Economics,
Federal-Provincial Affairs

	Expenditure
1970-71	146,021
1971-72	166,123

Ministry of Treasury, Economics and Intergovernmental Affairs,
Economic Policy and Intergovernmental Affairs

1972-73	1,952,660
1973-74	2,160,684
1974-75	2,807,087
1975-76	2,407,563
1976-77	4,260,113

Intergovernmental Affairs

1977-78	1,796,204

	Ministry of Intergovernmental Affairs	Intergovernmental Relations Branch
1978-79	510,924,698	1,060,144
1979-80	686,805,709	1,564,295
1980-81	463,170,498	1,407,022
1981-82	5,436,696	1,969,965
1982-83	7,222,921	4,172,695
1983-84	6,865,106	3,896,116
1984-85	8,030,281*	4,850,400*

*Estimates

Personnel[5]

	Employees
1979	197
1980	195
1981	243
1982	50
1983	62
1984	68

EXTERNAL OFFICES

The MIA operates three international offices:

- Brussels, Belgium
- Paris, France
- Frankfurt, Germany

The Ontario government also has external offices in London, Hong Kong, China, Japan, as well as in several American cities, including Boston, Chicago, New York, Los Angeles, Dallas and Atlanta. These offices are all operated by the Ministry of Industry, Trade, and Technology.

INTERGOVERNMENTAL UNITS IN OTHER DEPARTMENTS

Ministry of Treasury and Economics
  Intergovernmental Finance Policy Branch

Ministry of the Environment
  Intergovernmental Relations and Enforcement Division

Notes

1. Government of Ontario, *Telephone Directory*, Autumn, 1985.
2. "Ministry of Intergovernmental Affairs", (pamphlet), 1983.
3. "Ministry of Intergovernmental Affairs", (pamphlet), 1985.
4. 1970-71 to 1983-84: *Public Accounts*, Ministry of Treasury and Economics, various years. 1984-85: *Expenditure Estimates*, 1984-85.
5. *Annual Report*, Civil Service Commission, various years.

PRINCE EDWARD ISLAND

Cabinet Office

1985 ORGANIZATION

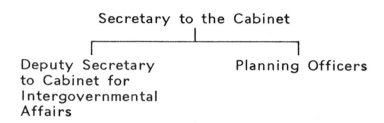

Secretary to the Cabinet

Deputy Secretary to Cabinet for Intergovernmental Affairs

Planning Officers

HISTORY

Although a separate intergovernmental affairs office was not established in the Prince Edward Island government until 1979, an important step was taken 10 years earlier. In 1969, the Department of Development was created to manage a long-term umbrella agreement reached with the federal government. This agreement, the Comprehensive Development Plan, was divided into three phases. Until it was disbanded in 1980 – following the second phase – the Department of Development was responsible for the management of the Plan.

An Intergovernmental Affairs Office was established in the Executive Council Office in 1979, where it existed until 1983. It operated under a cabinet directive with no statutory provisions. In 1980, responsibility for management of the Development Plan was transferred to the newly-created Intergovernmental Affairs Office.

A reorganization in 1983 transferred the functions of this Office to the Cabinet Office. The Cabinet Office, which had been established in 1981, provides the research and policy analysis support for the Cabinet and its committees. "Intergovernmental Affairs" operates as a separate unit within the Cabinet Office. It has a staff of two people. The Deputy Secretary to Cabinet for Intergovernmental Affairs – working in the Cabinet Office – acts as secretary to the Cabinet Committee on Intergovernmental Affairs.

MANDATE

The primary role of the Intergovernmental Affairs Office (1979 to 1983), and of the intergovernmental affairs unit currently in the Cabinet Office, is to ensure that the Province of Prince Edward Island presents coordinated positions in negotiations with both the federal and other provincial governments. Much of the work involves preparation for First Ministers' Conferences and Premiers' Conferences. Initially, the Office of Intergovernmental Affairs was largely concerned with the negotiations surrounding the patriation of the constitution.

The Intergovernmental Affairs Office provided operational support to the various Cabinet Committees in relation to the monitoring of departmental relations with other governments. It was responsible for ensuring that matters surrounding intergovernmental negotiations or consultations were addressed by the Cabinet Committees or Executive Council, as required. These functions are now performed by personnel in the Cabinet Office.

Regional development agreements with the federal government remain a primary concern for the intergovernmental specialists in the Cabinet Office. The Deputy Secretary to Cabinet for Intergovernmental Affairs, working in the Cabinet Office, is the provincial official responsible for coordinating the negotiation of subsidiary agreements with the federal government under the umbrella Economic and Regional Development Agreement (ERDA), reached in 1984.

RESOURCES

Financial[1]
Intergovernmental Affairs Office, Executive Council
1979-80	3,625
1981-82	57,575
1982-83	158,056

INTERGOVERNMENTAL UNITS OTHER DEPARTMENTS

Department of Finance
   Federal-Provincial Fiscal Relations

Department of Industry
   Federal-Provincial Division

Notes

1. *Public Accounts of the Province of Prince Edward Island,* various years.

QUEBEC

Secrétariat aux affaires intergouvernementales canadiennes

1985 ORGANIZATION

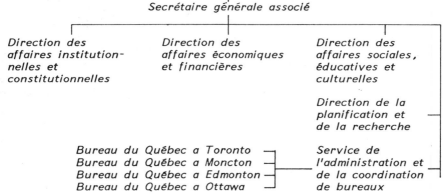

Ministre délégué aux affaires intergouvernementales canadiennes

Secrétaire générale associé

Direction des affaires institution-nelles et constitutionnelles

Direction des affaires économiques et financières

Direction des affaires sociales, éducatives et culturelles

Direction de la planification et de la recherche

Bureau du Québec a Toronto
Bureau du Québec a Moncton
Bureau du Québec a Edmonton
Bureau du Québec a Ottawa

Service de l'administration et de la coordination de bureaux

HISTORY
The *Ministère des affaires fédérales-provinciales* was created in March 1961. In 1967, the name of the Department was changed to *Ministère des affaires intergouvernementales*. On December 24, 1974, the Department came under new legislation, which strengthened the mandate of the Department and enhanced the authority of the Minister of Intergovernmental Affairs in all matters involving other governments. Also in 1974, the *Ministère des affaires intergouvernementales* was divided into three divisions: *Direction générale des affaires canadiennes*; *Direction générale des affaires internationales*; and *Direction générale de l'administration*.

In 1984, the *Ministère des affaires intergouvernementales* was disbanded. The international side of the department was changed to become a separate department: *Ministère des relations internationales*. Relations with other governments in Canada became the responsibility of the *Secrétariat aux affaires intergouvernementales canadiennes*, located in the *Ministère du conseil exécutif*. The *Secrétariat* is headed by a *Secrétaire générale associé* and is responsible to a *Ministre délégué aux affaires intergouvernementales canadiennes*.

There are currently three policy-oriented branches: *Direction des affaires institutionnelles et constitutionnelles*; *Direction des affaires économiques et financières*; and *Direction des affaires sociales, éducatives et culturelles*. As well, there exists a *Direction de la planification et de la recherche* and a *Service de l'administration et de la coordination de bureaux*.

STATUTES

An Act to establish the Department of Federal-Provincial Affairs, 1961
This Act provided for the Minister of Federal-Provincial Affairs to direct the Department. He was to attend to all necessary relations between the Quebec government and the governments of Canada and the other provinces. He was to "promote the full realization of provincial autonomy and further intergovernmental collaboration in compliance with the constitution."[1] He was unable to make any agreement without the authorization of the Lieutenant-Governor in Council.

An Act to Amend the Federal-Provincial Affairs Department Act and Certain Related Acts, 1967
This Act provided for the change in the name of the Department to the *Ministère des affaires intergouvernementales*. It also amended the sections concerning the duties of the Minister, such that he was to coordinate all activities of the government outside Quebec, and those of its departments and bodies. "He

shall attend to all relations that may exist between the Quebec government, its departments and bodies, and other governments or bodies outside Quebec, and to the negotiation of agreements which may be made with such governments or bodies, in conformity with the interests and rights of Quebec."[2]

Concerning intergovernmental agreements, the Minister still required the authorization of the Lieutenant-Governor in Council. It was possible that such authorization be granted to the Minister even in cases where a law provides that a person other than he may make such an agreement.

Intergovernmental Affairs Department Act, 1974
This Act provided for the appointment of a Deputy Minister. As well, it expanded the responsibilities of the Minister to include: the elaboration and proposing to the Government of external relations policy and the implementation of such policy adopted by the Government; the establishment and maintenance of such relations with other governments and their departments and the coordination of all activities of the Government outside the province; the promotion of the cultural, economic and social development of the people of Quebec by the establishment of intergovernmental relations; responsibility for official communications between the Government of Quebec, other governments and international organizations; ensuring that the constitutional jurisdiction of the province is respected and the participation of Quebec in the preparation and implementation of federal policies and programmes affecting the development of Quebec; cooperation with the other departments for the implementation of policies outside Quebec.

The Minister was to oversee the negotiation of all intergovernmental agreements and their implementation. To be valid, intergovernmental agreements had to be approved by the Lieutenant-Governor in Council and be signed by the Minister.

The Act prohibited any official from taking a position in the name of the Government at an intergovernmental meeting unless he had received an express mandate for such purpose given under the authority of the Minister.

An Act to Amend Various Legislation, 1984
This statute amended, among others, the Act Respecting the *Ministère du conseil executif*. It provided for the creation of a "Canadian Intergovernmental Affairs" division. It gave to the Premier or the Minister designated by the Government essentially the same powers which had been granted to the Minister of Intergovernmental Affairs in earlier statutes.

MANDATE

The *Ministère des affaires intergouvernementales* was originally created for the purpose of coordinating Quebec's federal-provincial relations. Statutory changes in 1974 greatly enhanced the role of the Department and its minister. The primary focus of the Department changed from simply performing a monitoring role to one involving greater control. Virtually all interaction with other governments had to be done with the knowledge and approval of the Minister. Also in 1974, a *Direction des affaires internationales* was established. Over the subsequent ten years, international relations became a primary focus of the Department.

The branch responsible for Canadian affairs, originally located in the Department of Intergovernmental Affairs and now in the *Ministère du conseil exécutif,* is responsible for the coordination of Quebec's activities in its relations with the federal government and the other provinces. Personnel in this agency are grouped according to sector. They work in concert with the corresponding sectoral departments, and contribute to the negotiation of intergovernmental agreements.

The *Secrétariat aux affaires intergouvernementales canadiennes* is subdivided into primarily three branches: *Direction des affaires économiques et financières; Direction des affaires sociales, éducatives et culturelles;* and *Direction des affaires institutionnelles et de la recherche.*[3]

The *Direction des affaires institutionnelles et de la recherche* is concerned with constitutional matters and the long-term focus and direction of Quebec's intergovernmental relations in the Canadian context. The *Direction des affaires économiques et financières* ensures the coordination of policies in a variety of sectors, including natural resources, agriculture, regional development, and environment.

The *Direction des affaires sociales, éducatives et culturelles* is concerned with various sectors in the social and cultural realms, including: health care, communications, justice, language, aboriginal affairs, and immigration. There also exists a newly-created *Service de l'administration et de la coordination de bureaux*, which oversees the Quebec's *bureaux* that are located in other provinces. This branch is also responsible for Quebec's relations with francophones in other provinces.

RESOURCES

Financial[4]

	Ministère des affaires intergouvernementales Expenditure	Direction générale des affaires canadiennes Expenditure
1977-78	30,150,000	1,396,000
1978-79	36,644,000	2,809,000
1979-80	42,312,000	3,003,000
1980-81	46,990,000	3,767,000
1981-82	44,774,000	3,795,000
1982-83	46,514,000	4,075,000
1983-84	49,246,000	4,121,000

Secrétariat aux affaires intergouvernementales canadiennes

1984-85	4,592,100*
1985-86	6,799,900*

*Estimates

Personnel[5]

	Ministère des affaires intergouvernementales Employees	Direction générale des affaires canadiennes Employees
1977-78	414	48
1978-79	438	47
as of:		
March 31, 1979	462	46
March 31, 1980	471	57
March 31, 1981	444	55
March 31, 1982	432	51
March 31, 1983	423	50
March 31, 1984	370	43

EXTERNAL OFFICES

The Government of Quebec has three offices in other Canadian provinces, as well as an office in Ottawa.

Moncton: opened in 1980, for the industrial promotion of Quebec products and businesses
Toronto: opened May 8, 1982.
Edmonton: opened in May 1982.
Ottawa: opened in the spring of 1984.

The Quebec government also has several offices in other countries; these are under the direction of the *Ministère des relations internationales*.

INTERGOVERNMENTAL UNITS IN OTHER DEPARTMENTS

Ministère des finances
    Direction des relations financières intergouverne-mentales

Ministère de la main-d'oeuvre et de la securité du revenu
    Direction des affaires extra-ministérielles

160

Ministère de l'éducation
   Direction des relations extérieures

Ministère de la santé et des services sociaux
   Etentes fédérales-provinciales

Ministère des affaires culturelles
   Service des relations intergouvernementales

Ministère du travail
   Affaires extra-ministérielle

Ministère des transport
   Relations extra-ministérielle

Notes

1. Section 2.
2. Section 2.
3. Summarized in *Rapport annuel 1982-83, Ministère des affaires intergouvernementales*, 1984, p. 10.
4. *Comptes publics*, various years, and *Rapports annuels, Ministère des affaires inter- gouvernementales*, various years.
5. *Rapports annuels, Ministère des affaires inter- gouvernementales*, various years.

SASKATCHEWAN

Intergovernmental Affairs Branch,
Executive Council Office

1985 ORGANIZATION

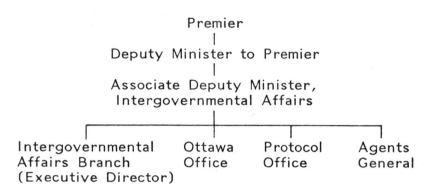

Premier
|
Deputy Minister to Premier
|
Associate Deputy Minister,
Intergovernmental Affairs
|

| Intergovernmental Affairs Branch (Executive Director) | Ottawa Office | Protocol Office | Agents General |

HISTORY

In 1974, an Intergovernmental Affairs unit was established in the Planning and Research Branch of the Executive Council Office. In 1977, a separate Office of Intergovernmental Affairs was established. Two years later, a new Department was charged with performing this function.

The Department of Intergovernmental Affairs existed from 1979 to 1983. There were initially three branches: Constitutional Branch; International Affairs Branch; and Intergovernmental Co-ordination Branch. The Intergovernmental Coordination Branch had three major functions:

1. to coordinate the intergovernmental relations of the Province of Saskatchewan;
2. to negotiate intergovernmental agreements;
3. to monitor intergovernmental relations. [1]

In 1980-81, a reorganization expanded the Department to include the Protocol office and the Office of the Agent General (London). Also included were the Grants to

Planning and Research Institutes. In November 1982, the Communications Policy Branch and the Indian and Native Affairs Branch became part of the Department. The Communications Policy Branch dealt with issues in telecommunications, cable and broadcasting and communications technologies.

In 1983, the Department of Intergovernmental Relations was disbanded. The constitutional affairs branch was put into the Department of Justice and the Indian and Native Affairs Branch became a separate secretariat. The Communications Policy Branch became a new communications secretariat attached to the Minister of Justice. Responsibility for grants to the Saskatchewan Council for International Cooperation was transferred to the Department of Agriculture.

The other activities moved to the Executive Council Office. Since 1983, the Intergovernmental Affairs (formerly Intergovernmental Cooperation) Branch in the Executive Council Office has assumed the key coordinating role for intergovernmental affairs in Saskatchewan. It is headed by an Executive Director. An Associate Deputy Minister to the Premier for intergovernmental affairs was appointed in February 1984. Besides the Intergovernmental Affairs Branch, the Protocol Office and the Ottawa Office report to the Associate Deputy Minister.

STATUTES

An Act to establish the Department of Intergovernmental Affairs, 1979
The Act created the Department of Intergovernmental Affairs and provided for the appointment of a deputy minister.

The Minister of Intergovernmental Affairs was to be responsible for the coordination of, and for making recommendations to the Executive Council on, all policies, programs and activities of the Government of Saskatchewan and its agencies in relation to any other government. As well, he was to continually review all such policies and activities of the government, all intergovernmental agreements, and all relevant legislation. The Act stipulated that he may be a party to the negotiation of proposed intergovernmental agreements, take action to initiate or maintain intergovernmental cooperation, and establish offices outside the province that are necessary for the establishment and maintenance of intergovernmental cooperation.

The Act stipulated that the Minister be informed of the negotiation of every proposed intergovernmental agreement and be sent a copy of each proposed agreement before it is executed. The minister was deemed to be authorized to negotiate the terms of intergovernmental agreements. However, the statute stated that failure to comply with the provisions of this section with respect to any intergovernmental agreement did not render the agreement inoperative.

An Act to amend the Department of Intergovernmental Affairs Act, 1981
A few minor revisions were made to the Act, including the limiting of the power of the minister with respect to the establishment of offices outside the province.

An Act to repeal the Department of Intergovernmental Affairs Act, 1983
This act provided for the disbanding of the Department of Intergovernmental Affairs.

An Act respecting the Consequential Amendment Resulting from the Reorganization of the Structure of the Government of Saskatchewan (Bill 32), 1983
Section 47 amends the Legislative Assembly and Executive Council Act. Among the changes, the Department of Executive Council assumed certain functions, including the coordination of intergovernmental affairs, responsibility for the Ottawa Office, and the administration of the Agent-General's office in London.

MANDATE

During the years of the constitutional negotiations, a separate department was seen as essential, both to provide the constitutional support to the Premier and to have a minister who could participate in the negotiations in lieu of the Premier. The end of the constitutional process in 1982 coincided with a change in government in Saskatchewan.

The new government felt that its intergovernmental objectives could best be achieved by having an agency responsible for intergovernmental affairs located in the Executive Council Office rather than a separate department. Interactions between the Government of Saskatchewan and other governments — which are necessary if the government is to pursue its priority interests and to achieve its specific objectives — must be effectively planned, co-ordinated and managed. These activities are the responsibility of the Intergovernmental Affairs Branch. It provides a unique contribution within government.

- the ability to link initiatives within the province with those of other jurisdictions in order to enhance the deliverability of the province's objectives;
- a thorough and up-to-date knowledge of the relative priorities and positions on individual issues of other governments;
- the full corporate view of the government's relative priorities on intergovernmental issues across all sectors.

In pursuit of these objectives the branch must carry out the following activities:

- to ensure that the Government is fully informed on a timely basis of existing and emerging trends, events and opportunities or constraints to the achievement of the Government's objectives.
- to be fully informed of all issues and concerns and of all existing and planned programs and policies of all departments within the Government.
- to assist the Government (Cabinet) to articulate and priorize its policy and program objectives in its interactions with other governments.

- to ensure that all strategic instruments available to the Government in the field of intergovernmental relations are used to their maximum effectiveness in the achievement of the Government's objectives.
- to ensure that the priorized objectives of the Government in the field of intergovernmental affairs are pursued effectively and achieved promptly through the Government's interactions with other governments.

RESOURCES

Financial[2]

Intergovernmental Affairs, Executive Council

	Expenditure
1978-79	47,982.08
1979-80	92,025.37

	Department of Intergovernmental Affairs	Intergovernmental Co-ordination Branch
1979-80	622,105.86	125,376.85
1980-81	1,963,349.10	236,691.86
1981-82	1,855,684.93	286,316.27
1982-83	4,940,688.50	297,014.00

Intergovernmental Affairs Branch, Executive Council

1983-84	563,057.42
1984-85	718,960*
1985-86	755,180*

*Estimates

Personnel[3]

Department of Intergovernmental Relations

	Permanent Person-Years
1979-80	18
1980-81	26
1981-82	28.8
1982-83	29.5[4]

Intergovernmental Affairs Branch, Executive Council
    1983-84   14
    1984-85   14

EXTERNAL OFFICES

London, England
The Office of the Agent General in London was established in 1948. From 1980 until 1983, it was under the auspices of the Department of Intergovernmental Affairs. Currently, it is responsible to the Associate Deputy Minister, Intergovernmental Affairs.

Ottawa
Opened in August 1980, the principal functions of this office are to provide a continuing liaison between the Saskatchewan government and the offices of federal Cabinet ministers, and to ensure effective communication between the Saskatchewan government and the federal administration in Ottawa. One aspect of this liaison is to ensure that Saskatchewan's points of view are fully considered in the development of federal policy iniatives. From 1980 until 1983, it was under the auspices of the Department of Intergovernmental Affairs. Currently, it is responsible to the Associate Deputy Minister, Intergovernmental Affairs.

INTERGOVERNMENTAL UNITS IN OTHER DEPARTMENTS

Department of Finance
    Taxation and Economic Policy

Saskatchewan Social Services
    Federal-Provincial Arrangements Branch

Notes

1. *Annual Report*, 1981-82. Saskatchewan Inter-governmental Affairs, 1983.
2. 1978-79 to 1983-84: *Public Accounts*, various years. 1984-85 to 1985-86: *Estimates*, various years.
3. *Estimates*, various years.
4. When all the components of the Department of Intergovernmental Affairs (including Communications Policy, Indian and Native Affairs, Agent General, Co-ordination, etc.) were combined, the number of person-years in the *Estimates* jumped to 65.9.

NORTHWEST TERRITORIES

Department of the Executive

1985 ORGANIZATION

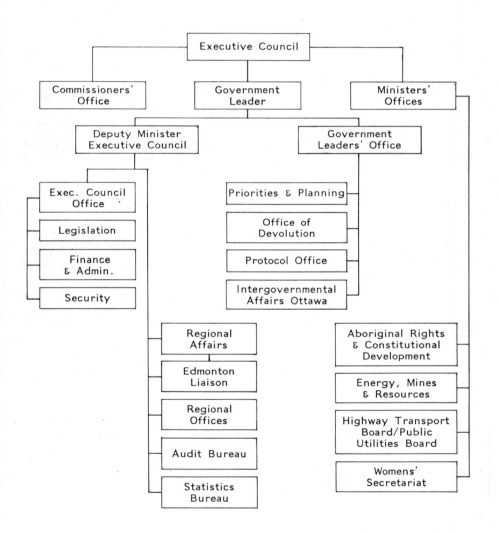

HISTORY

The Department of the Executive was created in 1980 to improve the efficiency of the Cabinet decision-making system, as well as to improve internal coordination on issues requiring a total government approach in the Government of Northwest Territories. Related structures include an Aboriginal Rights and Constitutional Development Secretariat and, since August 1985, an Office of Devolution. Both are part of the Department of Executive.

The responsibility for Intergovernmental Affairs has recently been assigned to the Government Leader's Office, reporting to the Government Leader through the Principal Secretary. The Intergovernmental Affairs Office consists of a Liaison Office in Ottawa and a Protocol Office in Yellowknife.

MANDATE

The Northwest Territories Government has a very decentralized approach to intergovernmental relations. The Intergovermental Affairs Office is not a true central coordinating body, but rather acts as a service agency in assisting departments when requested to arrange meetings, representing departments at official functions, preparing briefings and carrying out other duties as requested.

EXTERNAL OFFICES

Ottawa
The Ottawa office was established in 1980. It is the main intergovernmental affairs agency for the Government of the Northwest Territories. It employs two people.

YUKON

Policy and Intergovernmental Relations Branch,
Executive Council Office

1985 ORGANIZATION

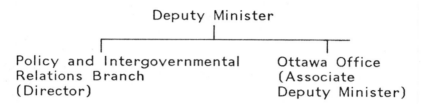

Executive Council Office

Deputy Minister

Policy and Intergovernmental
Relations Branch
(Director)

Ottawa Office
(Associate
Deputy Minister)

HISTORY

The Directorate of Intergovernmental Affairs was established in the early 1970s as part of Administrative Services, a body responsible for providing administrative support to the Yukon Legislative Council, the Commissioner, and the Executive Committee. In 1978, this Directorate became part of the Executive Council Office.

In 1979, as a result of action initiated by the federal Minister of Indian Affairs and Northern Development, profound changes were made in the structure and operation of the Yukon government. Portfolio responsibilities, including Intergovernmental Affairs, previously held by the Commissioner were assumed by the Government Leader.

The Department of Intergovernmental Relations was formed in April 1981 through the amalgamation of the pipeline branch, land claims secretariat, and the Directorate of Intergovernmental Affairs. In June 1982, this Department joined with the Department of Economic Development to become the Department of Economic Development and Intergovernmental Relations.

On July 1, 1983, Intergovernmental Relations was transferred to the Executive Council Office. It is now the "Policy and Intergovernmental Relations Branch". In addition to its intergovernmental work, the Branch provides a policy analysis and policy coordination service. The Director chairs the Policy committee and also serves as Deputy Secretary to Cabinet.

MANDATE

The Policy and Intergovernmental Relations Branch is responsible for reviewing all intergovernmental relations involving the Yukon Government. It is concerned with broad issues, such as constitutional developments, the move toward devolution, and the transfer of responsibilities from the federal government.

This Branch fulfills a support role for the Government Leader in his intergovernmental functions. This includes preparation for First Ministers' Conferences and Annual Premiers' Conferences. The Branch reviews all intergovernmental agreements and participates in intergovernmental meetings. It is also responsible for protocol duties on behalf of the Yukon Government.

Coordination is an important part of this Branch's mandate. It coordinates or directs projects that have implications across the government as opposed to those that are only of interest to one or two departments. In this sense the Branch offers an intragovernmental service. The projects do not necessarily have intergovernmental implications. Current projects concern official bilingualism in the Yukon and science and technology policy.

RESOURCES

Financial[1]
Intergovernmental Affairs,
Administrative Services Office

	Expenditure (Estimates)
1975-76	109,570
1976-77	132,637

172

Intergovernmental Affairs Directorate,
Executive Council Office
    1978-79   130,400
    1979-80   139,300
    1980-81   146,500

Department of Intergovernmental Relations
    1981-82   967,000

Department of Economic Development and
Intergovernmental Relations
    1982-83   1,646,000

Policy and Intergovernmental Relations Branch,
Executive Council Office
    1985-86   322,000

Personnel[2]
Intergovernmental Affairs Directorate
            Person-Years
            (Estimates)
    1978-79   3.25
    1979-80   3.25
    1980-81   3.25

Policy and Intergovernmental Relations Branch,
Executive Council Office
    1985-86   6

EXTERNAL OFFICES

Federal Relations Office, Ottawa
The primary responsibility of this Office is to act as a communications link between the Government of Yukon and the federal government. Although the Ottawa Office is a separate component, its budget is an activity under the Policy and Intergovernmental Relations Branch.
    1985-86 Budget: 222,000

INTERGOVERNMENTAL UNITS IN OTHER DEPARTMENTS

Department of Finance
In 1983, a Fiscal Relations Officer was attached to the Ottawa office to coordinate financial negotiations with the federal government on reaching an agreement for financing.

Notes

1. 1975-76 to 1980-81, 1985-86: *Main Estimates,* various years. 1981-82: "Revised Estimates", *Yukon Annual Report,* 1982, p. 27. 1982-83: "Revised Forecast", *Yukon Annual Report,* 1983, p. 25.
2. *Main Estimates,* various years.

BIBLIOGRAPHY

Adie, Robert F. and Thomas, Paul G. *Canadian Public Administration. Problematic Perspectives*, Scarborough: Prentice-Hall, 1982.

Aucoin, Peter. "The Expenditure Budget Process: Management Systems ad Political Priorities." in B. Jameieson, ed. *Governing Nova Scotia. Policies, Priorities and the 1984-85 Budget*. Halifax: School of Public Administration, Dalhousie University, 1985, 9-20.

Aucoin, Peter and Bakvis, Herman. "Regional Responsiveness and Government Organization: The Case of Regional Economic Development Policy in Canada." in P. Aucoin, ed. *Regional Responsiveness and the National Administrative State*. Toronto: University of Toronto Press (Volume 37, Royal Commission on the Economic Union and Development Prospects for Canada research study), 1985, 51-118.

Bernard, Louis. "La conjoncture actuelle des relations intergouvernementales." in R. Simeon, ed. *Confrontation and Collaboration - Intergovernmental Relations in Canada Today*. Toronto: The Institute of Public Adminstration of Canada, 1979, 99-104.

Black, Edwin R. and Cairns, Alan C. "A Different Perspective on Canadian Federalism." *Canadian Public Administration*, 9, 1966, 27-45.

Brown, Douglas and Eastman, Julia. *The Limits of Consultation. A Debate Among Ottawa, the Provinces and the Private Sector on an Industrial Strategy.* Ottawa: Science Council of Canada, 1981.

Bryden, Kenneth. "Cabinets." in Bellamy et al, ed. *The Provincial Political Systems. Comparative Essays.* Toronto: Methuen, 1976, 310-22.

Bryden, Kenneth. "Executive and legislature in Ontario: a case study on governmental reform." *Canadian Public Administration,* 18:2, 1975, 235-52.

Burns, R.M. *Intergovernmental Liaison on Fiscal and Economic Matters.* Kingston: Institute of Intergovernmental Relations, 1968.

Burns, R.M. "The Machinery of Federal-Provincial Relations:II" *Canadian Public Administration,* 8:4, December 1965, 527-34.

Cairns, Alan C. "The Other Crisis of Canadian Federalism." *Canadian Public Administration,* 22, 1979, 175-95.

Cairns, Alan C. "The Governments and Societies of Canadian Federalism." *Canadian Journal of Political Science,*X:4, 1977, 695-726.

Campbell, Colin and Szablowski, George. *The Superbureaucrats: Structure and Behaviour in Central Agencies.* Toronto: Macmillan of Canada, 1979.

Careless, Anthony. Initiative and Response. *The Adaptation of Canadian Federalism to Regional Economic Development.* Montreal: The Institute of Public Administration of Canada, 1977.

Careless, Anthony. "The Struggle for Jurisdiction: Regionalism versus Rationalism." *Publius. The Journal of Federalism,* 14:1, 1984, 61-78.

Clark, Ian D. "Recent Changes in the Cabinet Decision-making System in Ottawa." *Canadian Public Administration,* 28:2, 1985, 185-201.

Dobuzinskis, Laurent. "Rational Policy-Making: Policy, Politics, and Political Science." in T.A. Hockin, *Apex of Power, 2nd Edition,* Scarborough: Prentice-Hall, 1977, 211-28.

Doern, G. Bruce, "Horizontal and Vertical Portfolios in Government." in Doern and Wilson, ed. *Issues in*

Canadian Public Policy. Toronto: Macmillan of Canada, 1974, 310-36.

Doern, G. Bruce. "The Cabinet and Central Agencies." in Doern and Aucoin, ed. *Public Policy in Canada*. Toronto: the Macmillan Company of Canada, 1979, 27-61.

Doerr, Audrey. *The Machinery of Government in Canada*. Toronto: Methuen, 1981.

Doerr, Audrey. "Public Administration: Federalism and Intergovernmental Relations." in K. Kernaghan, ed. *Canadian Public Administration: Discipline and Profession*. Toronto: Butterworths, 1983, 122-37.

Dupre, J. Stefan. "Reflections on the Workability of Executive Federalism." in R. Simeon, ed. *Intergovernmental Relations*, Toronto: University of Toronto Press, (Vol. 63, Royal Commission on the Economic Union and Development Prospects for Canada research study), 1985, 1-32.

Esman, Milton J. "Federalism and Modernization: Canada and the United States." *Publius. The Journal of Federalism*, 14:1, 1984), 21-38.

Feldman, Elliot J. and Feldman, Lily G. "The Impact of Federalism on the Organization of Canadian Foreign Policy." *Publius. The Journal of Federalism*, 14:1, 1984, 33-59.

Gallant, Edgar. "The Machinery of Federal-Provincial Relations:1" *Canadian Public Administration*, 8:4, 1965, 515-26.

Gibbins, Roger. *Conflict and Unity. An Introduction to Canadian Political Life*. Toronto: Methuen, 1985.

Goodsell, Charles T. "The Role and Importance of Bureaucracy in Federal Systems." Prepared for the 1984 Annual Conference, Royal Australian Institute of Public Administration, Perth, Australia, November 1984.

Government of Alberta. *Annual Report*, Department of Federal and Intergovernmental Affairs, 1975 to 1984.

Government of British Columbia. *First Annual Report* Ministry of Intergovernmental Relations, 1981.

Government of Canada. "Progress Report on Federal-Provincial Relations." Prepared for the

Annual Conference of First Ministers, Halifax, November 28-29, 1985.

Government of Manitoba. *Report of the Task Force on Government Organization and Economy*, 31 March 1978.

Government of Quebec. *Rapport annuel*, Ministère des Affaires intergouvernementales, various years.

Government of Saskatchewan, *Annual Report 1981-82*, Saskatchewan Intergovernmental Affairs, 1982.

Jenkin, Michael. *The Challenge of Diversity. Industrial Policy in the Canadian Federation. Background Study No. 50*. Ottawa: Science Council of Canada, 1983.

Kernaghan, Kenneth. "Intergovernmental Administrative Relations in Canada." in K. Kernaghan, ed. *Public Administration in Canada, Selected Readings, 4th ed.*, Toronto: Methuen, 1982, 80-93.

Kernaghan, Kenneth. "The Power and Responsibility of Intergovernmental Officials in Canada." prepared for the Annual Conference of the Institute of Public Administration of Canada, Winnipeg, August 1979.

Laframboise, H.L. "The Future of Public Administration in Canada." *Canadian Public Administration*, 25, 1982, 507-19.

Leeson, Howard. "Accommodative Mechanisms in a Decentralizing Federation: The Intergovernmental Affairs Function in Saskatchewan." Presented to the Institute for Public Administration, St. John's, August 1985.

Léger, Paul C. "The Cabinet Committee System of Policy-making and Resource Allocation in the Government of New Brunswick." *Canadian Public Administration*, 26:1, 1983, 16-35.

Mallory, J.R. "The Two Clerks: Parliamentary Discussion of the Role of the Privy Council Office." *Canadian Journal of Political Science*, X:1, 1977, 3-20.

Meekison, J. Peter. "First ministers' Conferences in the Canadian Federal System." in T. Courchene et al, ed. *Ottawa and the Provinces: The Distribution of Money and Power. Volume 2*. Toronto: Ontario Economic Council, 1985, 162-82.

Report of the Royal Commission on the Economic Union and Development Prospects for Canada, Volume 3, Ottawa: Ministry of Supply and Services, 1985.

Ruff, Norman J. "British Columbia and Canadian Federalism." in J.T. Morley et al. *The Reins of Power. Governing British Columbia.* Vancouver: Douglas and McIntyre, 1983, 271-305.

Sabetti, Filippo & Waller, Harold M. "Crisis and Continuity in Canadian Federalism." *Publius. The Journal of Federalism,* 14:1, 1984, 1-8.

Savoie, Donald J. "The GDA Approach and the Bureaucratization of Provincial Governments in the Atlantic Provinces." *Canadian Public Administration,* 24:1, 1981, 116-32.

Savoie, Donald J. *Regional Economic Development: Canada's Search for Solutions,* Toronto: University of Toronto Press, 1986.

Savoie, Donald. "The Continuing Struggle for a Regional Development Policy" in P.M. Leslie, ed. *Canada: The State of the Federation 1985,* Kingston: Institute of Intergovernmental Relations, 1985, 135-50.

Schultz, Richard. "Prime Ministerial Government, Central Agencies, and Operating Departments: Towards a More Realistic Analysis." in T.A. Hockin, ed. *Apex of Power. The Prime Minister and Political Leadership in Canada, 2nd. Edition.* Scarborough: Prentice-Hall of Canada Limited, 1977, 229-36.

Simeon, James C. "Policy-Making in the Cabinet." in D.C. MacDonald, ed. *The Government and Politics of Ontario,* Toronto: Van Nostrand Reinhold Ltd, 1980, 102-22.

Simeon, Richard. *Federal-Provincial Diplomacy: The Making of Recent Policy in Canada,* Toronto: University of Toronto Press, 1972.

Simeon, Richard. *The Federal-Provincial Decision Making Process. Intergovernmental Relations. Issues and Alternatives* 1977. Toronto: Ontario Economic Council, 1977.

Simeon, Richard. *Intergovernmental Relations and the Challenges to Canadian Federalism.* Prepared for the Conference of the Institute of Public Administration, Winnipeg, August 1979. Kingston: Institute of Intergovernmental Relations, 1979.

Simeon, Richard. "Intergovernmental Relations in Canada Today - Summary of Discussions." in R. Simeon, ed.

Confrontation and Collaboration - Intergovernmental Relations in Canada Today. Toronto: The Institute of Public Administration of Canada, 1979. pp. 1-16

Simeon, Richard. "Natural Resource Revenues and Canadian Federalism: A Survey of the Issues." *Canadian Public Policy*, 6, 1980.

Smiley, Donald V. "An Outsider's Observations of Federal-Provincial Relations among Consenting Adults." in R. Simeon, ed. *Confrontation and Collaboration - Intergovernmental Relations in Canada Today.* Toronto: The Institute of Public Administration of Canada, 1979, 105-113.

Smiley, Donald V. "Public Administration and Canadian Federalism." in J. P. Meekison, ed. *Canadian Federalism: Myth or Reality?*, Toronto: Methuen, 1968, 271-86.

Smiley, D.V. "Federal-Provincial Conflict in Canada." *Publius: the Journal of Federalism.* 4:3, 1974, 7-24.

Smiley, Donald V. *Constitutional Adaptation and Canadian Federalism Since 1945.* Document of the Royal Commission on Bilingualism and Biculturalism, no. 4. Ottawa:Information Canada, 1970.

Smiley, Donald V. *Canada in Question: Federalism in the Eighties. Third Edition.* Toronto: McGraw-Hill Ryerson, 1980.

Smiley, Donald V. "Public Sector Politics, Modernization and Federalism: The Canadian and American Experiences." *Publius. The Journal of Federalism,* 14:1, 1984, 39-60.

Sproule-Jones, Mark. "The Enduring Colony? Political Institutions and Political Science in Canada." *Publius. The Journal of Federalism,* 14:1, 1984, 93-108.

Stevenson, Don. "The Role of Intergovernmental Conferences in the Decision-making Process." in R. Simeon, ed. *Confrontation and Collaboration - Intergovernmental Relations in Canada Today.* Toronto: The Institute of Public Administration of Canada, 1979, 89-98.

Stevenson, Garth. *Unfulfilled Union. Canadian Federalism and National Unity. Revised Edition,* Toronto: Gage Publishing Ltd., 1982.

Swainson, Neil A. "The Public Service." in J.T. Morley et al. *The Reins of Power. Governing British Columbia*. Vancouver: Douglas and McIntyre, 1983, 119-60.

Tennant, P. "The NDP Government of British Columbia: Unaided Politicians in an Unaided Cabinet." *Canadian Public Policy*, III:4, 1977, 489-503.

Thorburn, Hugh G. *Planning and the Economy. Building Federal-Provincial Consensus*. Ottawa: Canadian Institute for Economic Policy, 1984.

Van Loon, R. "Planning in the Eighties." in French and Van Loon, *How Ottawa Decides, Second Edition*, Toronto: Lorimer and Co., 1984, 157-90.

Van Loon and Whittington, *The Canadian Political System. Environment, Structure, and Process. Third Edition*. Toronto: McGraw-Hill Ryerson Limited, 1981.

Veilleux, Gérard. "Federal-Provincial Administrative Relations in Canada." in K. Kernaghan, ed. *Bureaucracy in Canadian Government. Second Edition*. Toronto: Methuen, 1973, 138-43.

Veilleux, Gérard. "L'évolution des mécanismes de liaison intergouvernementale." in R. Simeon, ed. *Confrontation and Collaboration - Intergovernmental Relations in Canada Today*. Toronto: The Institute of Public Administration of Canada, 1979, 35-77.

Veilleux, Gérard. *Les Relations Intergouvernementales au Canada 1867-1967*, Montreal: Les presses de l'université du québec, 1971.

Veilleux, Gérard. "Intergovernmental Canada: Government by Conference? A Fiscal and Economic Perspective." *Canadian Public Administration*, 23, 1980, 33-53.

Wallace, Donald C. "Provincial Central Agencies for Intergovernmental Relations and the Policy Process," (unpublished Ph.D dissertation, York University), October 1985.

Warhurst, John. "Intergovernmental Managers and Co-operative Federalism: The Australian Case." *Public Administration*, 61, 1983, 308-17.

Willms, A.M. "The Executive and the Departmental Structure." in K. Kernaghan, ed. *Public*

Administration in Canada. Selected Readings, 3rd Edition. Toronto: Methuen, 1977, 54-8.

Wilson, V. Seymour. "Federal-Provincial Relations and Federal-Policy Processes, in Doern and Aucoin, ed. *Public Policy in Canada*. Toronto: the Macmillan Company of Canada, 1979, 190-212.

Woolstencroft, Timothy Bryn. "Intergovernmental Emissaries - The Provincial Guardians of the Federal Bargain: A Case Study of Alberta and Ontario" (unpublished M.A. thesis, Queen's University), 1980.

Woolstencroft, Timothy B. *Organizing Intergovernmental Relations*. Kingston: Institute of Intergovernmental Relations, 1982.

Young, Walter D. and Morley, J. Terence. "The Premier and the Cabinet." in J.T. Morley et al. *The Reins of Power. Governing British Columbia*. Vancouver: Douglas and McIntyre, 1983, 45-82.

Young, R.A., Faucher, Phillipe, Blais, Andre. "The Concept of Province-Building: A Critique." *Canadian Journal of Political Science*, XVII:4, 1984, 783-818.

LIST OF TITLES IN PRINT

Peter M. Leslie, editor, *Canada: The State of the Federation 1985*, 1985. ($14)

Peter M. Leslie, *Politics, Policy, and Federalism: Defining the Role of the Institute of Intergovernmental Relations*, 1984. ($7)

Catherine A. Murray, *Managing Diversity: Federal-Provincial Collaboration and the Committee on Extension of Services to Northern and Remote Communities*, 1984. ($19)

Peter Russell *et al*, *The Court and the Constitution: Comments on the Supreme Court Reference on Constitutional Amendment*, 1982. (Paper $7, Cloth $15)

The Year in Review

Bruce G. Pollard, *The Year in Review 1983: Intergovernmental Relations in Canada*. ($16)

Revue de l'année 1983: les relations intergouvernementales au Canada. ($16)

S.M. Dunn, *The Year in Review 1982: Intergovernmental Relations in Canada*. ($12)

Revue de l'année 1982: les relations intergouvernementales au Canada. ($12)

S.M. Dunn, *The Year in Review 1981: Intergovernmental Relations in Canada*. ($10)

R.J. Zukowsky, *Intergovernmental Relations in Canada: The Year in Review 1980, Volume I: Policy and Politics*. ($8) (*Volume II not available*)

D. Brown, *Intergovernmental Relations in Canada: The Year in Review 1979*. ($7)

Queen's Studies on the Canadian Communities

Keith Banting, *The Welfare State and Canadian Federalism*, 1982. (Published with McGill-Queen's University Press. Distributed by University of Toronto Press.)
Allan Tupper, *Public Money in the Private Sector: Industrial Assistance Policy and Canadian Federalism*, 1982. ($12)
William P. Irvine, *Does Canada Need a New Electoral System?*, 1979. ($8)

Discussion Paper Series

22. Robert L. Stanfield, *National Political Parties and Regional Diversity*, 1985. (Charge for postage only)
21. Donald Smiley, *An Elected Senate for Canada? Clues from the Australian Experience*, 1985. ($8)
20. Nicholas Sidor, *Consumer Policy in the Canadian Federal State*, 1984. ($8)
19. Thomas Hueglin, *Federalism and Fragmentation: A Comparative View of Political Accommodation in Canada*, 1984. ($8)
18. Allan Tupper, *Bill S-31 and the Federalism of State Capitalism*, 1983. ($7)
17. Reginald Whitaker, *Federalism and Democratic Theory*, 1983. ($7)
16. Roger Gibbins, *Senate Reform: Moving Towards the Slippery Slope*, 1983. ($7)
15. Norman K. Zlotkin, *Unfinished Business: Aboriginal Peoples and the 1983 Constitutional Conference*, 1983. ($10)
14. John Whyte, *The Constitution and Natural Resource Revenues*, 1982. ($7)
13. Jack Mintz and Richard Simeon, *Conflict of Taste and Conflict of Claim in Federal Countries*, 1982. ($7)
12. Timothy Woolstencroft, *Organizing Intergovernmental Relations*, 1982. ($8)
10. Anthony Scott, *Divided Jurisdiction over Natural Resources*, 1980. ($6)

Bibliographies

Federalism and Intergovernmental Relations in Australia, Canada, the United States and Other Countries: A Bibliography, 1967. ($9)
A Supplementary Bibliography, 1975. ($10)
A Supplementary Bibliography, 1979. ($5)

Aboriginal Peoples and Constitutional Reform

PHASE ONE

Background Papers

1. Noel Lyon, *Aboriginal Self-Government: Rights of Citizenship and Access to Governmental Services*, 1984. ($10)
2. David A. Boisvert, *Forms of Aboriginal Self-Government*, 1985. ($10)
3. NOT AVAILABLE
4. Bradford Morse, *Aboriginal Self-Government in Australia and Canada*, 1985. ($10)
5. Douglas E. Sanders, *Aboriginal Self-Government in the United States*, 1985. ($10)
6. Bryan P. Schwartz, *First Principles: Constitutional Reform with Respect to the Aboriginal Peoples of Canada 1982-1984*, 1985. ($15)

Discussion Paper

David C. Hawkes, *Aboriginal Self-Government: What Does It Mean?*, 1985. ($10)
Set ($60)

PHASE TWO

Background Papers

7. David C. Hawkes, *Negotiating Aboriginal Self-Government, Developments Surrounding the 1985 First Ministers' Conference*, 1985. ($5)
8. John Weinstein, *Options for Aboriginal Self-Government off a Land Base*, May 1986.
9. Bradford W. Morse, *How Landless Aboriginal Peoples Can Obtain Land and Resources, and on What Terms and Conditions*, May 1986.
10. Richard Bartlett, *Aboriginal Self-Government of Land and Resources in Canada*, May 1986.
11. Jerald E. Paquette, *Aboriginal Self-Government in the Field of Education*, May 1986.
12. Mark Malone, *Financing Aboriginal Self-Government*, May 1986.
13. C.E.S. Franks, *Public Administration Questions in Aboriginal Self-Government*, May 1986.
14. William T. Badcock, *Legal and Constitutional Issues Involved in Implementing Aboriginal Self-Government Agreements*, May 1986.
15. Delia Opekokew, *Economic and Political Inequity Among Aboriginal Peoples*, October 1986.
16. *How Great a Financial Burden, if any, Might be Imposed on Existing Governments (Federal, Provincial, Territorial, Municipal) Should Aboriginal Self-Government Receive Constitutional Recognition*, October 1986.
17. *Problems of Jurisdiction and Policy Co-ordination Which Might Arise, and How These Can Be Minimized, Should Aboriginal Self-Government Be Constitutionally Recognized*, October 1986.
18. David C. Hawkes, *Aboriginal Self-Government and the Section 37 Negotiations*, July 1987.

Position Papers

1. *Aboriginal Self-Government*, A position paper by the Assembly of First Nations, May 1986.

2. *Aboriginal Self-Government*, A position paper by the Inuit Committee on National Issues, May 1986.
3. *Aboriginal Self-Government*, A position paper by the Native Council of Canada, May 1986.
4. *Aboriginal Self-Government*, A position paper by the Metis National Council, May 1986.

Discussion Paper

David C. Hawkes, *Possibilities for Accommodation at the 1987 First Ministers' Conference on Aboriginal Constitutional Matters*, December 1986.

Bibliography

Bibliography on Aboriginal Self-Government in Canada September 1986.

Publications may be ordered from:
Institute of Intergovernmental Relations
Queen's University
Kingston, Canada
K7L 3N6